Religion in context

Religious power assumes many strikingly different forms, which are often regarded both by believers and by students of religion as unique, unrelated, and even mutually exclusive. In this book, however, I. M. Lewis adopts a holistic approach and argues that to understand the nature of spiritual power we need to appreciate how these apparently contradictory mystical manifestations are in fact part of a single complex of mutually defining and sustaining elements. Stressing the importance of rigorous social contextualization, he analyzes such seemingly disparate phenomena as spirit-possession, witchcraft, cannibalism, and shamanism, which are usually attributed to separate cults and even cultures, revealing the interconnections both between them and with the world religions, such as Islam and Christianity.

Besides presenting a critique of the treatment of religious phenomena as reified, Professor Lewis demonstrates – in an intriguing deconstruction of the classic anthropological fieldwork situation that he sees as itself a kind of shamanic initiation – the complexity of the problem of understanding other people's beliefs, and the way in which these beliefs often inadvertently become part of anthropological theory. He emphasizes the continuing strength in social and cultural anthropology of a comparative approach that constantly seeks to force anthropological "theory" into a dialogue with ethnographic particulars, thereby encouraging the distillation of empirically more satisfactory theory.

This illumination of critical aspects of religious power, a demonstration of the value of a comparative approach in the formulation of anthropological theory, will interest scholars and students of social and cultural anthropology and religious studies, as well as other readers concerned with the nature of religion in the modern world.

Religion in context

Cults and charisma

I. M. Lewis
London School of Economics and Political Science

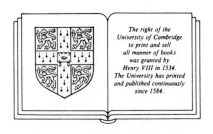

Cambridge University Press

Cambridge
London   New York   New Rochelle
Melbourne   Sydney

Published by the Press Syndicate of the University of Cambridge
The Pitt Building, Trumpington Street, Cambridge CB2 1RP
32 East 57th Street, New York, NY 10022, USA
10 Stamford Road, Oakleigh, Melbourne 3166, Australia

First Published 1986
Reprinted 1987

Printed in the United States of America

Library of Congress Cataloging in Publication Data
Lewis, I.M.

Religion in context

Bibliography: p.

1. Cults – Addresses, essays, lectures.
2. Religions – Addresses, essays, lectures.   3. Witchcraft
– Addresses, essays, lectures.   4. Cannibalism – Addresses,
essays, lectures.   5. Shamanism – Addresses, essays,
lectures.   6. Anthropology – Addresses, essays,
lectures.   I. Title
BL80.2.L48   1986   291   85 – 14935

British Library Cataloguing in Publication Data
Lewis, I.M.

Religion in context: cults and charisma.

1. Cults
I. Title
306'.6   GN470

ISBN 0 521 30616 7 hard covers
ISBN 0 521 31596 4 paperback

Contents

Preface	*page*	vii
Acknowledgments		xi
1.	Anthropological fieldwork and the context of belief	1
2.	Possession cults in context	23
3.	Witchcraft within and without	51
4.	The cannibal's cauldron	63
5.	The shaman's career	78
6.	The power of the past: African "survivals" in Islam	94
Notes		108
Bibliography		118
Index		133

Preface

The beliefs and behavior conventionally distinguished as "witch-craft," "spirit-possession," "cannibalism," and "shamanism" seem at first sight to have little in common. Anthropologists and other students of comparative religion regularly treat these phenomena as totally unrelated and even mutually exclusive, objectified "things" characteristic of different cults and of distinct types (and stages) of culture and society. This book takes a different view. It argues that, on the contrary, these are actually closely related expressions of mystical power, or "charisma." In fact, as we shall see when we examine them closely, each illuminates the others, and the integrative, comparative approach advocated here enables us to understand how the conquest and transformation of malign forces ("negative charisma") empowers the leaders of charismatic cults, whose status is always potentially ambiguous. Especially where they occupy a marginal position in relation to a world religion, such cults of affliction are frequently stigmatized in their wider social context as "superstitious survivals." Our analysis indicates that, on the contrary, such cults are often recent developments and, by attributing the unorthodox to the past, actually play a crucial role in the definition of orthodox belief itself.

In endeavoring to elucidate these contrasting configurations of mystical power by emphasizing their underlying interconnections rather than their differences, I also seek to display the continuing value in social (and cultural) anthropology of a comparative analysis – one that continually seeks to force anthropological "theory" into a dialogue with ethnographic "facts," encouraging the distillation of empirically more satisfactory theory. This empiricist dialogue is indeed complex, as I emphasize in the opening chapter, which reflects upon anthropological fieldwork itself as a form of shamanistic initiation. Questioning the glib anthropological construction of culturally representative "cosmologies," Chapter 1 explores the origins of "anthropological" theories of witchcraft and their relation to native beliefs and disbeliefs. The standard psychodynamic, social-tension theory of witchcraft as an expression of jealousy and spite is, as we see, borrowed directly from the native sources to which it is applied by anthropologists. This in turn offers an illuminating epidemiological perspective for understanding the incidence of those afflictions affecting particularly women, which are interpreted in terms of spirit-possession and which involve spirits that indirectly exert pressure on the opposite sex. Hence the anthropological theory of witchcraft, derived from ethnographic sources, also helps us to understand and analyze the ethnography of spirit-possession.

The plight of such innocent female victims of spirit attack, who are hardly to blame for their vulnerability, suggests intriguing analogies to that recalcitrant case in witchcraft studies – the self-confessing, involuntary witch. Such "introvert" self-accusing witches, who often turn out to be women desperately seeking help, are like their spirit-possessed counterparts in effect mystically licensed to exert pressure on their immediate circle. Thus by applying the theory of witchcraft analysis to spirit-possession, we gain new insights into witchcraft itself. This prompts the general reconsideration we embark upon in Chapter 3 of types of witchcraft (and sorcery) as modes of mystical attack, suggesting that spirit-possession and "introspective witchcraft" are milder forms of mystical aggression, employed against superiors, than are "extrovert" accusations, directed against inferiors. The limiting factor here is apparently that possession cult charismatic leaders risk denunciation as witches.

This anthropological understanding of the dynamics of witchcraft and spirit-possession is informed by the generally disbelieving stance of the anthropologist. This has had, as we see in Chapter 4, a curious effect on anthropological studies of cannibalism, where reports of cannibalism in witchcraft contexts have been dismissed as fantasy while often being uncritically accepted in non-witchcraft contexts! Here the cannibalistic reputation acquired by Europeans in colonial Africa after their suppression of witchcraft (and, hence, inadvertent protection of witches) should give us pause. A more enlightening approach to the meaning of cannibalism as ideology or practice acknowledges this relationship with witchcraft and takes the analysis of mystical power one stage farther, stressing its connection with the various modes of sexual aggression.

Although, as I emphasize, it is never unambiguously so, in all these contexts mystical power is seen primarily as a negative force. The dramatic conquest of this malign power is, however, as Chapter 5 insists, the archetypal foundation for the assumption of the charismatic role par excellence – that of the shaman. This is the most positive meaning placed upon affliction as the basis for initiation into charismatic cults. As soon as the treatment takes the form of domestication rather than exorcism, it becomes a charismatic initiation rite of the type central to shamanism. As I argue, misleading reifications that treat "positive" and "negative" mystical experience separately have prevented anthropologists and others from appreciating the ubiquitous character of shamanistic initiation and its position in the "career structure" of spirit-possession cults. Ethnographic data again force us to revise anthropological theory.

As well as providing a better understanding of the internal dynamics of charismatic cults, this cumulative comparative analysis also highlights the external role of marginal cults in the broader definition of ideological boundaries. My final chapter shows (with reference to African Islam) how these marginal, local cults are classified officially (against the historical evidence) as "survivals" and so contribute to the dynamic process of adjustment by which universal world religions define and redefine metropolitan orthodoxy by contrasting it to "primitive superstition." The price centrality pays to marginality for providing this service is, in effect, the ambiguous power it cedes to the latter. This dialectical context forces us to scrutinize carefully the concept of "survival" and prompts at the same time a better understanding of the nature and needs of orthodoxy. It also takes our analysis of the precipitating circumstances of women's peripheral spirit-possession a stage farther, showing how the extent of the involvement of wives in these cults may become an index of *embourgeoisement* and male respectability and so become linked to the changing status of women. And here, for the moment at any rate, I rest my case. At least I hope to have demonstrated the advantages of this general comparative approach to configurations of mystical energy that are usually reified and treated as though they had no connection with one another – and so are, as I argue, gravely misunderstood.

Chapters 1 and 2, based on formal public lectures, have been left essentially in the form in which they were originally delivered, issues raised by Chapter 2 and subsequent developments being elaborated in the following chapters. In revising this latter material particularly, I have benefited from discussions with a wide range of colleagues and friends at the universities of Budapest, Helsinki, Illinois, Indiana, Kyoto, Naples, Osaka, Pennsylvania, Rome, Urbino, and Washington (to mention only the more distant). As usual, I am especially grateful to Joan Wells, Caroline Simpson, and Carol Evans for typing (and retyping) so much of this book. Christina Toren's help in systematizing and checking the notes and bibliography is also warmly appreciated.

Acknowledgments

Chapter 1 is based on an inaugural lecture, "The Anthropologist's Muse," delivered at the London School of Economics on October 17, 1973.

Chapter 2 is an edited version of the Malinowski Memorial Lecture for 1966, originally published in *Man* 1, no. 3 (1966):307–25.

Chapter 3 is a revised version of "A Structural Approach to Witchcraft and Spirit Possession," originally published in M. Douglas, ed., *Witchcraft Confessions and Accusations* (London, Tavistock, 1970), pp. 293–310.

Chapter 4 is an expanded version of a lecture given at the Laboratoire Peiresc (Valbonne) and at the Universities of Urbino and Kyoto, and printed in abbreviated form in *Research: Contributions to Interdisciplinary Anthropology* 2 (1983):39–50.

Chapter 5 is an extended version of a paper, "What is a Shaman?," originally published in *Folk* 23 (1981):25–36.

Chapter 6 developed from a lecture first given at Accademia dei Lincei (Rome, 1981) and later published in *Temenos* 19 (1983):55–67.

The author thanks the editors of these publications for permission to reprint this material in its revised form here.

1

Anthropological fieldwork and the context of belief

I

Those who are not social or cultural anthropologists must be surprised at the deep metaphysical significance we attach to fieldwork in exotic settings as a necessary condition in our formation and continued existence as practicing anthropologists. Malinowski's patron and the first regular teacher of our subject at the London School of Economics, Professor C. G. Seligman, did not exaggerate when he eloquently pleaded for research funds with the words "Field research in anthropology is what the blood of the martyrs is to the Church."[1] If only the one had flowed as freely as the other! It makes us what we are: Without it we are nothing. So, if you ask most students why they want to study anthropology, you will be told disarmingly, "To do fieldwork." And if you are so ill-advised as to attend a staff meeting in any university anthropology department, you will be amazed at the rancorous clamor that breaks out as soon as we reach that perennial agenda item, our competing claims to apply for leave to carry out further research overseas.

Fieldwork thus is our Utopia, our millennial dream. In such an atmosphere mere "library research," as it is disparagingly described, is virtually taboo – a possibility, perhaps, for lame ducks and rainy days. The ultimate test of the professional anthropologist's standing remains the successful completion of a major piece of field research in exotic surroundings. It is necessary also for the researcher to display an impressive command of the relevant vernacular and present the results of his heroic endeavors in an appropriately detailed and scholarly monograph where they can be carefully scrutinized. The more difficult, dangerous, and inaccessible the terrain, the better. Similarly, the longer the period of fieldwork, the greater the student's merit. So the number of years and months (and sometimes even weeks) notched under the sun is studiously logged and scrutinized by our recording angels. These statistics are carefully preserved and figure prominently in that fascinating ethnographic document, *The Register of Members of the Association of Social Anthropologists of the Commonwealth*.[2]

In this tradition, the most damaging criticism that can be lodged against a colleague concerns the quality of his fieldwork. Did he *really* get the facts right? Did he *really* speak the local language with sufficient proficiency for us to accept his complicated interpretations of their symbols? Do his findings represent a view biased by his close association with only one section of the community he studied? Suspicions of this sort dog the reputations, and sometimes threaten the careers, of even the most dazzling theoreticians if they have not also given acceptable proof of their scholarship as fieldworkers. Here Lévi-Strauss's case is particularly interesting. As he himself sometimes admits and as his warmest British advocates acknowledge,[3] his field research is patchy and thin and falls far short of the standards Malinowski established. Indeed, most of his theoretical writing relies heavily on information collected by other anthropologists and is in this sense markedly dependent on secondary sources. Yet he proclaims the crucial role of fieldwork for our subject and exhibits highly ambivalent attitudes toward it. Replying to a spirited attack by the French sociologist Gurvitch, Lévi-Strauss accuses the latter of misunderstanding and exaggerating the aims of anthropology. We do not, he retorts loftily, attempt to reach as complete a knowledge as possible of the societies we study. And he continues, "The disparity between such an ambition and the resources available to us is so great that we might be called charlatans, and with good reason. How would one penetrate the dynamics of an alien society after a stay of a few months, knowing nothing of its history, and usually very little of its language?"[4]

This interesting riposte, to which it is tempting to rejoin, "Speak for yourself," contrasts sharply with another passage by the same author. Here, again in reply to Gurvitch, Lévi-Strauss parades by name the various ethnic groups he has visited in South America and protests indignantly, "All these names are associated with men and women of whom I have been fond, whom I have respected, whose faces remain in my memory. They remind me of joys, hardships, weariness and, sometimes, dangers. *These are my witness* [emphasis supplied], the living link between my theoretical views and reality."[5] And in a later passage, he announces even more insistently, perhaps even defiantly, "I am an anthropologist who has conducted fieldwork."[6] This is not the image of Lévi-Strauss with which we are most familiar, but it is one of the many facets of his intriguing situation to which I shall return later. We may also note here how one of the currently most influential schools of American anthropology makes a similar and more direct fetish of fieldwork through its slogan, "New Ethnography." By this title it seeks to appropriate the prestige that traditionally attaches to the most minutely detailed and scrupulous collection of field data.

As further evidence of the anthropologist's obsession with fieldwork in alien cultures, the peculiar position of the anthropologist who investigates his own culture merits attention. As one would expect, orthodox opinion holds that such research is of dubious legitimacy. The distance between the observer and the observed is not considered sufficiently wide to generate those sparks of intercultural inspiration so essential to the anthropological imagination. Yet is this always and necessarily so? Few societies are truly homogeneous. Most contain significant and to some degree mutually incomprehensible cultural distinctions. This is one reason why it is perfectly possible for a British patrial to carry out authentic anthropological field research within the United Kingdom. Ulster is perhaps a rather extreme example of such a setting. There is also the consideration that the autochthonous anthropologist in a sense often does his fieldwork in reverse. The imaginative leaps in such cases occur not so much in the actual collection of the ethnographic data as in the analysis and writing-up.

Finally, if fieldwork is crucial in our subject, different methods of doing it should produce different kinds of anthropology. In a sense, this has always been a dominant assumption, one that underlies the great importance we all attach to Malinowski's influence. In this vein, Audrey Richards[7] has pointed out how the contrasting characteristics of French and British anthropology reflect their different modes of fieldwork. The light-footed French descend in droves like locusts upon their terrain, making a succession of short, sharp probes. These may be continued at intervals over a decade or more and sometimes culminate in a sudden final climactic confrontation when the peoples they study at last submit to this relentless goading and expose their hidden souls. How different we British anthropologists are! Our approach is solitary, more intensive and concentrated as we doggedly attempt to unravel and record for posterity the dominant features of a whole culture in eighteen to twenty-four months of uninterrupted work and total immersion in the world of our hosts. We share the same Muse as our French colleagues, but we practice her rites in a different style.

Through this romantic quest for knowledge and illumination from the uncharted peoples of the Third World – those for the most part traditionally neglected by more conventional European scholarship – social anthropology can legitimately claim to stand as the authentic founder of black studies, the original academic discipline devoted to the study of alternative cultures, institutions, and beliefs. We are thus true transcultural transvestites, professional aliens, cross-cultural voyeurs. And fieldwork is primarily a matter of observation and detection, so that abundant natural curiosity is an essential attribute of the successful research worker. Whether he likes it or not, every anthropologist is in practice a private eye, prying relentlessly and often irritatingly into the affairs of his foreign hosts and so intruding savagely on their privacy. No wonder most anthropologists, whatever their intentions, political opinions, or connections, are regarded at some stage in fieldwork as spies. (There is a curious harmony between this sinister aspect of the most empirical part of anthropology and the current fashion that terms such as "hidden messages," "codes" to be "cracked," and other jargon borrowings from the communications industry enjoy in that rarefied world of symbolic analysis known to its intimates, a little unfortunately perhaps, as semiology.) Such indeed is the field-worker's privileged intimacy with his informants that, if we are to follow some authorities, it automatically rules out marriage as well as other, less formal romantic attachments. So, according to Margaret Mead, one of the particular hazards likely to arise in studying what she somewhat old-fashionedly calls "high cultures" is the danger that the anthropologist might actually want to marry his or her informants![8]

II

Fieldwork is for us also a voyage in a different sense, since it is the royal road to the anthropological calling. The would-be anthropologist trains for fieldwork, disappears into the field, and finally returns to write up the research, collect a Ph.D., and embark upon a professional career. As a number of anthropologists have noticed, and none more perceptively than Rosemary Firth,[9] we see here the familiar tripartite structure common to most transition rituals. In the first phase, the neophyte prepares to surrender his old status and to shed ethnocentric assumptions. In the second, "liminal" phase, he retires to learn the new culture of his hosts. In the third phase, he re-emerges to be readopted within his own academic culture in a new role as professional anthropologist. Each stage has its attendant traumas, which have to a certain extent become conventionalized, the most taxing being those of the actual field research and subsequent writing-up. Here, however, there is a deep paradox. In its factual and theoretical concerns, anthropology is a cumulative discipline in which new discoveries give rise to new theories and these in turn engender novel research projects. Yet, the actual field experience is for each new recruit a unique and often regressive personal drama. This can be prepared for, but its full impact can never be precisely estimated in advance, nor can one say with complete confidence what the outcome will be.

These considerations, and the clearly critical significance of what we now know as "culture shock," naturally invite comparison to similar experiences in psychiatry and psychoanalysis.[10] There is certainly a valid sense in which "the field" is our equivalent of the analyst's couch, and the analogy between fieldwork and a training analysis is obvious. It is also not difficult to see that the process of participant observation implies at least partial assimilation and internalization of the morality and assumptions of the alien society under study. S. T. Kimball, for instance, records how he encountered a ghost in the course of his fieldwork in Ireland, and how this helped to convince his hosts that he was a normal human being. I remember, too, how impressed I was when Paul Baxter told me how he had become so thoroughly imbued with the spirit of the Boran pastoralists he was studying in northern Kenya that he began to have Boran dreams. Similarly, Rosemary Firth reports how on the eve of her departure from Malaya, where she had been working with her husband, Raymond, she had a terrifying nightmare. She dreamed that she had become "a Malay peasant, a woman crouching over the fire to blow up the embers for an evening meal." She awoke, she records, "in terror, momentarily confused about her own identity – Malay woman or English scientist."[11]

Much of the terminology employed in the more reflective writing about fieldwork carries the same allusions. Evans-Pritchard (my teacher at Oxford) tells us that only the anthropologist, and not his hosts, can make the "transference" that is essential if fieldwork is to be successful.[12] The burden of anthropological discussion on this point, however, seems rather to follow Lévi-Strauss[13] in regarding the anthropologist as the equivalent of the analyst or psychiatrist, and the people studied as patients. Thus the onus of transference is shifted from the anthropologist to the people under study. But we need not be too perturbed by these strange transformations, for even psychoanalysts now officially recognize what they engagingly call "countertransference." This is the well-known process by which the analyst develops feelings toward the patients that are as ambivalent as their own toward the analyst. We also know, of course, that the boundary between patient and practitioner is, in the psychiatric field especially, not always clearly defined, and indeed is readily crossed in either direction.

These facts are more explicitly recognized in that older deviant cult that anthropologists call spirit-possession or shamanism, which I find a more illuminating model for both the psychoanalytic and the anthropological professions. Consider the parallels.[14] Like shamans, anthropologists go on trips to distant and mysterious worlds from which they bring back rich stores of exotic wisdom. They mediate between their own group and the unknown. They speak "with tongues" that are often unintelligible at home, and they act as mediums for the alien cultures through which they roam and which, in a sense, they come to incarnate. Like so many shamans or psychiatrists, they regularly occupy marginal positions in their own cultures as well as in those they visit in search of knowledge.

Again, as was Malinowski, anthropologists are typically summoned suddenly and dramatically from other occupations and impelled to assume their true and final calling. Malinowski's whole system of graduate anthropological training was based on the shamanistic assumption that all his students were converts, inspired by Providence to enter into their true destiny. And this method was transferred lock, stock, and barrel to Oxford, where it was administered first by Radcliffe-Brown and then by Evans-Pritchard. This shamanistic tradition survives in the influentially held view (which I do not entirely share) that social anthropology should only be taught at the graduate level to mature students who have already been trained in another discipline.

Pursuing my parallel, we should note that in internalizing the culture of the alien hosts (as their client) the anthropologist becomes possessed by them. True, in common with shamans the world over, the anthropologist may dissemble and claim that he "possesses them," speaking suspiciously often of *"his* people." But do not be deceived. The real situation is that they possess him. Or rather, as in other possession cults, the situation is in reality ambiguous, each participant possessing the other (as in sexual intercourse). Finally, as the anthropologist proceeds to analyze and write up his findings, he externalizes his experience and gradually disengages himself from his informants. He reestablishes the original distance separating the two cultures. This process is a form of exorcism. And, as one would expect, as in shamanistic cults, the anthropologist rarely achieves a final and complete separation from his Muse. He instead remains in a permanent state of bondage, periodically seized and impelled to further bouts of exorcistic writing. Some, alas, are denied even this relief and remain so completely enthralled that they defy all attempts at exorcism, subsisting in what is virtually a perpetual state of mute communion with their Muse.

III

It is now time to begin our careful scrutiny of the treasures that the anthropologist brings back from his shamanistic voyages. First, what psychiatrists would doubtless identify as our "primary" gains. If he had not acquired new information about a hitherto unrecorded or underrecorded culture, the anthropologist would have little to say. For, of course, we are all plagiarists, *bricoleurs,* living parasitically upon our ethnographic sources. Where would Malinowski have got without the Trobriand Islanders, Evans-Pritchard without the Nuer and Zande, Firth without the Tikopia, or Forde without the Yako? All our pronouncements carry conviction and authenticity only when we anchor them in the lives and thoughts of those we study. Our ethnographic sources provide our indispensable claims to legitimacy; they establish our credentials: "The Nuer do that, you say"; "How odd, the Somali don't"; and so on.

This ultimate referring of all our ideas to the ethnographic "facts" elucidated by painstaking field research is now so deeply engrained in our subject and so taken for granted that we tend to forget how dependent we are on our sources. Acutely aware of the subjectivity of our research techniques, we tend now to overestimate our part and to underestimate that of our informants. Strange as it may seem, the same tendency toward a position of ethnocentric superiority seems to me implicit in the rather overworked view of anthropology as the spoiled child of Western imperialism. Here those anthropologists who carried out research in the colonial territories are depicted as the deliberate – or, more charitably, unwitting – instruments of imperialism. These circumstances, it is held, have led those who undertook their fieldwork during that period to misunderstand the real position of their subjects and thus to have produced inevitably distorted analyses of social structures and cultures.

I find the condescending implications of this interpretation repugnant. It assumes that the people we study, or have studied, possess no vigor of their own; that they have insipid lackluster cultures with no intrinsic dynamism, no élan vital, no capacity for self-expression; and that such articulate representatives as anthropologists encounter are by definition not representative but, on the contrary, brainwashed slaves and Uncle Toms. Those who paint this misleading picture, it must be acknowledged, have usually not carried out actual fieldwork and tend to overgeneralize from the deplorable treatment of the American Indians in North and South America.[15] But they are also, I think, victims of a wider ethnocentric tendency to exaggerate greatly the force and finality of European culture and its implicit as well as explicit assumptions. Whatever Durkheim may have said, the people we study are *not* robots. Unlike artists' models, they do not posture pliantly as the omniscient ethnographer wields his brilliant brush. Cultures do *not* pose as "models" for the anthropologist in the servile, manipulable fashion that artists typically expect of their subjects. Excessive preoccupation with so-called theoretical models conceals, very conveniently, our own lack of originality and the contrasting richness of the peoples we study. It is *we*, not *they*, who are the puppets. Let me offer some evidence to support this heterodox view.

First let us take the instructive case of Lévi-Strauss. There exists a large and often tedious exegetical (I almost said liturigcal) literature on this brilliant man's thoughts and their intellectual pedigree (much of which he himself has disowned).[16] But whatever the obvious influences of Hegel, Marx, and Freud on the development of Lévi-Strauss's ideas, there is also a quite remarkable concordance between his key concepts and the salient characteristics of the ethnographic area in which he has actually carried out field research. As is well known, the colonial history of the American Indians is a sorry tale of rapacious exploitation and extermination. Those Indians who were not killed outright by the conquerors had their numbers dramatically reduced by exotic new diseases and related calamities. The surviving remnants of indigenous culture were then further impoverished and diluted by foreign accretions, with which in some cases they combined to produce bizarre hybrids. The presence today of Indian themes in the increasingly popular syncretic cults of the American continent bears impressive witness both to the vitality and persistence of Indian culture and to the centuries of intense pressure its authentic bearers have been forced to endure. Counterculture is a much older phenomenon in America than is generally supposed.

From the anthropological point of view, the colonization of America thus produced a bewildering assortment of ethnographic jigsaw puzzles. This encouraged those who sought to solve them to concentrate on what Robert Murphy has called the "cultural residues of the mind," as they attempted to wring out the last pieces of remembered custom from the oldest Indian informants they could find. As Murphy observes, it also prompted the publication of a series of monographs that, in their exhaustive cataloguing of disparate and often disjointed cultural elements, read like laundry lists.[17] These circumstances strikingly reflect Robert Lowie's famous definition of civilization as a "thing of shreds and patches."[18] They also, I suggest, directly reflect Lévi-Strauss's conception of primitives as *bricoleurs,* wayward beachcombers picking up and ingeniously recombining the strangely assorted treasures deposited on the sands by the successive tides of different cultures and civilizations. The same formative forces seem equally influential in the development of Lévi-Strauss's concepts of structure and structuralism and in his confusing contrast between what he calls "mechanical" and "statistical" models. An area so littered with various marinaded culture elements, and belonging as much to archaeology as to ethnography, prompted an earlier generation of anthropologists to explain the similarities between one culture-complex and another in terms of diffusion from a common original source. It is a very small step indeed from this to the cerebral geology of Lévi-Strauss and his quest for "unconscious structures," and one that fits the conditions of the area just as closely as the earlier diffusionist approach. Indeed, this transformation from diffusionism to structuralism is virtually explicit in some of the great master's writing.[19]

Let me turn now to examples of the same ethnographic imperialism from the British tradition of structural-functionalism. In recent years it has become increasingly evident that the theoretical interests of Africanist anthropologists – particularly their emphasis on corporate kinship groups, segmentary lineage systems, and centralized kingdoms – reflect local African cultural particularities. Generalizing theoretical models based on this work do not always travel as well as many had hoped. As Anthony Forge demonstrated so effectively in his 1971 Malinowski Lecture, New Guinea is in many respects a test case for anthropological theory. Difficulties over the importation there of Africanist models that have clearly suffered on the long sea-crossing sharpen our growing awareness of the extent to which much of our theorizing is influenced by the areas in which we carry out research.[20] Ah, those treacherous coral reefs! Similar compatibility problems arise when other ethnographic regions join the debate. It is now pretty clear, for instance, that the long controversy between Meyer Fortes and Edmund Leach at Cambridge over the relative significance of ties based on descent and those created by marriage is in large measure an issue between the Tallensi of northern Ghana and the Kachins of Burma. The former project an image of the ineluctable nature of kinship in blood. The latter are essentially alliance theorists who suppose that because in their case it is more honorable, and therefore more prestigious, to give than to receive wives, so it must be for all mankind. (The Kachins are, of course, mistaken on this point, as a number of Leach's colleagues have not hesitated to point out.)

But perhaps the most striking examples of this process in the *belle époque* of British social anthropology derive from the work of Evans-Pritchard and reflect his charisma as a teacher. Thus the lineages he discovered in the minds of the Nuer of the Sudan have been transported around the globe by his disciples and students. In the same way, the contrast he found in Zande conceptions between witch-craft as a psychic force and sorcery as a magical technique has assumed the status of a universally valid categorical distinction, one that has been applied indiscriminately elsewhere. It is also one of the cornerstones of several fashionable anthropological theories of religion and cosmology. The plain fact is, however, that most reli-gions that include analogous beliefs in mystical malevolence do not make the Zande distinction, which is actually the exception rather than the rule. Are there no limits, one might ask, to Zande cultural imperialism?

It will be evident, I hope, that although diffusionism may have withered away as an acceptable theoretical pursuit, like other ban-ished ghosts it still haunts the minds of anthropologists. It is, in fact, the main mechanism by which the cultures we study in one place influence what our students search for in another. To an important extent, anthropology is indeed the "translation of cul-ture," in the sense that the anthropologist picks up ideas in one place and unloads them in another. For this reason, following his own experience of two contrasting African cultures, Evans-Pritchard used to exhort his students to study more than one soci-ety. But even this may not suffice. So, with commendable candor, Max Gluckman confesses that his stimulating comparative analysis of rebellion in tribal states has been weakened by what he terms "the ethnocentrism bred by studying Zulu and Barotse."[21]

IV

Anthropological analyses, for all our fine talk, thus inevitably bear the stamp of the cultures in which they have been forged. But there is more to the plagiarism than this. It is not only what both the Dogon and Professor Lévi-Strauss would call "surface structures" that are thus appropriated and thrust into general theoretical cur-rency. We must also consider the role of what are sometimes known technically (and revealingly) as "key informants." Our dependence, at least in the elucidation of certain topics, on such figures is some-times explicitly acknowledged. So, for instance, Stanner describes the special relationship he developed with an Australian aborigine informant who was unusually gifted in employing homemade visual models to illustrate the structure of his society. Stanner reports how he eventually turned one of the old aborigine's demonstrations (in which sticks were used as counters and stick movements as signs of marriage, parentage, residence, and descent) into a model for teaching the theory of the aboriginal subsection system "much as they teach it."[22] With equal frankness, Raymond Firth records his debt to a particular Tikopia friend with whom he enjoyed a unique relationship and who contributed more than any other informant to his understanding of Tikopia society and culture. Anthony Forge pays similar tribute to the would-be Big-Man he encountered as a fellow stranger in the village that was his base in New Guinea, acknowledging the theoretical insight he gained from their discussions about the nature of power and authority among the Abelam.

Discounting Carlos Castaneda, the most outstanding examples on record of such fecund friendships with informants are almost certainly those of Victor Turner and Marcel Griaule; and they concern, as might be expected, the interpretation of religion and ritual. Turner's impressively documented analysis of the symbolism of the Ndembu people of central Africa is firmly anchored in a virtually unique apparatus of indigenous exegesis. This work is clearly based on months of painstaking observation and on commentaries from a multitude of independent sources obtained, wherever possible, in ritual contexts. Nevertheless, Turner has not hesitated to acknowledge his special debt to the magician Muchona (nicknamed "The Hornet"), who more than any other person guided him through the Ndembu forest of symbols. This imaginative interpreter of Ndembu symbolism and a friendly Ndembu mission teacher formed with Turner an impromptu field seminar or workshop, which, over a period of many months, pondered the inner mysteries of Ndembu religion and ritual. As Turner puts it, Muchona "delighted in making explicit what he had known subliminally about his own religion." Like his European colleague, but for different reasons, Muchona – who was frail, somewhat effeminate, and of slave origin – was in many respects an outsider, a marginal man capable of considering objectively what most Ndembu simply took for granted.[23]

Griaule's case is the more remarkable if for no other reason than that his dialogue with the blind Dogon sage Ogotommeli lasted thirty-three successive days and led to the production of that unique anthropological document, *Dieu d'Eau* (English version: *Conversations with Ogotommeli*). After fifteen years of intermittent research among this famous west African people of the Niger, it was Griaule's chance encounter with Ogotommeli that led to the final break-through into the inner mysteries of Dogon cosmology. In their sustained and highly sophisticated discussions, all the barriers separating the great French ethnographer and his brilliant *équipe* of younger workers from their final conquest of the deep structures of Dogon thought and myth were at last overcome. Ogotommeli himself died in 1947. He did not live to see either the book Griaule had written about him or the further progress of the French team's research. "His death," as Griaule sadly remarked at the time, was a "serious loss to humane studies." This tribute he was quick to qualify by adding, "not that the blind old man was the only one to know the doctrine of his people."[24]

Such examples illustrate the extent to which fieldwork is essentially a creative exchange. They also emphasize that it is a very unlucky field-worker who does not discover at least one local counterpart to help him with his task. These situations are, I believe, much more common than one might gather from much anthropological writing. Moreover, when they are acknowledged, the tendency is to present such encounters as exchanges in which the anthropologist inevitably plays the dominant role, so that the outcome cannot but be a tribute to his ingenuity and originality rather than to that of his informants. So, for instance, the suspicion lingers in many quarters that, having posed the appropriate philosophical questions, Griaule induced Ogotommeli to improvise an ad hoc philosophy, substantially a synthesis of elements from both their cultures rather than an authentic Dogon product. English commentators, at any rate, seem generally to see the result as a collaborative work of art in which it is difficult to disentangle the respective contributions of the two artists. This view recalls that enshrined in one splendidly egotistical passage in the first volume of *Mythologiques*, where Lévi-Strauss declares, "It is immaterial whether . . . the thought processes of the South American Indians take shape through the medium of my thought, or whether mine take place through the medium of theirs."[25]

V

Whatever the real balance of invention and creativity in these and comparable instances, we now turn to less obvious forms of anthropological plagiarism – cases in which, sometimes unwittingly, the ethnographer lifts from anonymous informants not only his many-layered factual data but also his *theoretical* interpretations. I begin with a case in which the interpretation is virtually explicit in the ethnographic "facts" themselves. It is much to her credit that Mary Douglas makes no attempt to disguise the ultimate ethnographic source of her contributions to anthropological theory. In the heady atmosphere of contemporary theorizing on the nature of cosmologies, however, it is often difficult to remember that the genesis of Douglas's stimulating ideas on dangerous anomalies reaches back, beyond William James and Leviticus, to the humble Lele of the Kasai in the Congo and to their taxonomic treatment of that fascinating creature, the scaly anteater (or, to be more accurate, of one of the two local varieties).[26] As Douglas records, the Lele describe the pangolin in such a way that there can be no "mistaking its anomalous character." The Lele say, "In our forest there is an animal with the body and tail of a fish, covered with scales. It has four legs, and it climbs on trees." It is also symbolically connected with fertility, being the object of a fertility cult, and in this context the Lele observe that like humans (but unlike other animals) the pangolin parsimoniously produces only one offspring at a time. So, as Mary Douglas points out, it is not difficult to see that pangolins are comparable to humans in the way that the overfecund parents of twins resemble animals. From this point of departure, Professor Douglas's fertile imagination moves quickly to the biblical abominations, on which she is able to shed new light, and thence to the more general explanatory concept of "matter out of place" (recalling Shaw's famous definition of obscenity), and finally to an elaborate general theory of mystical danger in which Lele ethnography is left far behind – for their ethnographer has, as it were, moved on and up into different intellectual circles. Those who disagree with her views may feel that the Lele have much to answer for!

Now to return to the work of Victor Turner among the Ndembu. Ndembu men pay their women the doubtful compliment of tracing all their important kinship links matrilineally. But in return they expect wives to leave their maternal kin and homes to live in the settlements of their husbands. This practice separates mature women from their nearest kin and especially from their brothers, for whom they provide heirs. These mundane events do not go unnoticed by the spirits. Women are regularly plagued by disease-bearing spirits that "catch" them, causing much inconvenience and suffering. Ndembu explain that the spirits strike their human prey because they are angry at being "forgotten," and in these circumstances it scarcely comes as a surprise to learn that the spirits involved are usually from the mother's side of the family. So, as Turner analytically expresses it, apparently paraphrasing the Ndembu, these women's spirit afflictions serve as a sharp and salutary reminder "that their own first loyalty is to their maternal villages and that they bear children not for their husbands but for their brothers back home."[27]

This example prompts consideration of a wider series of issues connected with the anthropologist's treatment of other people's mystical beliefs. As is well known, spirits and dreams are often loosely associated; indeed, one of the main Victorian intellectualist explanations for the existence of beliefs in spirits and spiritual activity traced their origin to dreams. The intellectual patent for this interpretation is usually, although not universally or unequivocally, assigned by anthropologists to Frazer's contemporary Sir Edward Tylor. Tylor's views on the subject, which have been widely condemned as absurdly simplistic, have passed into the anthropological literature only to pass out of it, with a few accompanying valedictory messages. Speaking for many of his colleagues, Evans-Pritchard castigates Tylor's theory as an explanation of the "if I were a horse" variety, the implication being that it was Tylor, not the savage, who made spirits out of dreams.[28] Even without psychoanalytic theory or the evidence of psychiatrists, however, there is actually a great mass of ethnographic data showing clearly and unambiguously that – with all due respect to Evans-Pritchard – Tylor's interpretation is, up to a point, good horse sense. Like so many of our own lay countrymen, the peoples we study do attach a great deal of importance to their dreams and explicitly adduce dream experience as evidence for the existence of the spirits in which they believe. This is ethnographic fact, not Tylorean fantasy.

Moreover, highly sophisticated subtleties are employed to create and sustain the links between dreams and spirits. Raymond Firth, for instance, speaking from a rationalist point of view, reports that the "Tikopia belief that the figure seen in a dream is not a human being but an impersonation of him by a spirit" disposes of naïve attempts to disprove the actuality of dreams by confronting the per-

son dreamed of with the contents of the dream.[29] (Godfrey Lienhardt's detailed account of the complex metaphysical significance
of dreams for the Dinka is also apposite here.)[30] The quotation
from Firth recalls the intriguing discussion between the Dogon phi-
losopher Ogotommeli and the French ethnographer Griaule on the
subject of the narrow steps of the Dogon heavenly house – how
could they possibly accommodate the vast numbers of animals their
cosmology required them to support? With its echoes of angels
dancing on pinheads, the question has a familiar ring; and so has
Ogotommeli's answer. As he explained, the animals involved were
all symbols, and "any number of symbols could find room on a
one-cubit step"![31]

Let us now turn to another area where there is an intriguing
interplay between mystical beliefs and anthropological theory. It is
generally recognized that one of the most impressive accomplish-
ments of anthropological analysis is its elucidation of the "problem
of witchcraft" – a subject Maurice Freedman has aptly described
as an "anthropologist's paradise." As we now understand, witchcraft provides an indispensable component in many philosophies of
misfortune. It is the friend rather than the foe of morality, which it
supports and even sometimes sanctions by attacking only those whose
moral imperfections expose them to its effects. And, in its actuali-
zation in witchcraft accusations, it offers a convenient means of
ventilating those pressures and tensions that are, as it were, part of
the opportunity cost of close-knit communal life everywhere. From
this perspective witchcraft is manifestly the pseudonym for jealousy
and envy, and the means by which these antisocial sentiments are
made to bear the burden of life's inequalities. These insights have
enabled anthropologists to achieve a deeper understanding of the
composite structure and complex workings of religion and ideology
generally. They also, of course, have corroborated much of the psychodynamic approach to interpersonal tensions in psychiatry – where
the terminology is a bit different, but the sentiments much the same.

This has not passed unnoticed. There is, nevertheless, a certain
irony in the position concerning this parallelism taken by some psychiatrists. Professor Ari Kiev, a leading American authority on the
subject, solemnly warns that, in view of the similarity between the
two theories, caution should be exercised in introducing the psychodynamic approach in certain cultures lest traditional witchcraft

beliefs be reinforced.[32] Some members of other disciplines are more accepting. A number of historians, and none more impressively than Keith Thomas and Alan MacFarlane, have taken these simple anthropological discoveries to heart and applied them effectively to many traditionally neglected and undervalued aspects of the beliefs of our own ancestors.[33] Those embarrassingly irrational superstitions of earlier generations gain a new lease on life when set in the wider context of meaning disclosed by anthropology.

My interest here, however, is simply in tracing the intellectual pedigree of these influential theories that attempt to explain witchcraft. The orthodox genealogy takes us back to Evans-Pritchard's analysis of Zande witchcraft[34] and to his remarkable mind – or perhaps more daringly to meetings between his mind and those of the Zande he knew well. But this is only half the story. We can go much farther and say that certain Zande – princes standing outside the vicious circle of witchcraft accusations, for instance, and other similarly detached informants – were as acutely aware as Evans-Pritchard of the scapegoating functions of witchcraft accusations and of the explanatory convenience of the beliefs themselves. Evans-Pritchard does not disguise this. Indeed, one of the most striking merits of his study lies precisely in his detailed examination and exposition of the points of convergence and divergence between his analysis of Zande beliefs and that made in different circumstances by various categories of Zande themselves. Other peoples with similar confidence in the efficacy of mystical malevolence have shown that they do not lag far behind the Zande or their ethnographer in appreciating what *really* underlies their beliefs.

I am not, of course, claiming that these indigenous analyses of the operation and significance of such major cultural phenomena as witchcraft beliefs necessarily coincide exactly with the "objective" picture that the anthropologist can elicit from a meticulous investigation of actual case histories. But I do hold that, at the very least, they constitute a kind of metatheory providing many essential clues, and that they are consequently the original, if modest, sources of much that passes for advanced anthropological theory.

Nor is it only in the field of witchcraft that our subjects are so gifted in self-analysis and so generous with their theoretical insights! Much the same often applies in the study of other religious phenomena. I once had the good fortune, for example, to meet a Somali tribesman who gave me an impeccably Durkheimian explanation of the function of the traditional ancestor cult in terms of the social euphoria generated by commemorative feasts at the ancestors' shrines (see Chapter 6). Again, it is not without significance that my interpretation of spirit-possession cults in terms of women's liberation (Chapter 2) partly derives from the manipulated men who have to bear most of the heavy costs and other inconveniences involved. Men's awareness of what their spirit-ridden wives are up to is, as will be shown, not limited to the Somali among whom I worked but seems to occur in most of the other officially male-dominated cultures where the same cults flourish.[35]

VI

These deeper instances of anthropological indebtedness raise two connected theoretical issues. The first and less significant, except methodologically, is the key importance of the skeptical informant who, being partly external to, or unconcerned in, a given situation, can stand back from it and take a more dispassionate, and in our terms "objective," view of what is happening. Skepticism clearly is not necessarily a full-time intellectual or emotional occupation. It is often simply a function of an individual's lack of direct involvement in particular circumstances. The wider and more interesting problem is that of determining, defining, and adequately describing what exactly it is that people do believe. If beliefs that ostensibly say one thing are widely understood to mean another, how do we assess them? How are we to price beliefs that regularly circulate at well below their face value? What is the relationship between the official and unofficial currencies, between the standard exchange rate and that on the black market? Where or when does belief become half-belief, and half-belief in turn become make-belief or dis-belief? Evans-Pritchard's exposition of Zande beliefs in witchcraft and magic will serve to clarify my difficulty. In a discussion that seems unconsciously to commemorate Freud, Evans-Pritchard shows clearly how Zande dispose of the problem created for them when their mystical techniques fail. Take a typical example: A witch doctor's diagnosis is falsified by subsequent developments. Zande conclude, very reasonably, that the doctor is an quack and should have his name struck off the register of authorized practictioners. He is no good because, obviously, he lacks sufficient knowledge of the mystical techniques necessary for effective work in his specialty. It is man, not magic, that is imperfect; and such particularistic confrontations between objective reality and the eternal Zande verities are, therefore, not of the kind to inaugurate scientific revolutions. Individual short-comings do not threaten general truths, which bounce back, as it were, with renewed vigor. Evans-Pritchard sums up this familiar situation in a succinct formula: faith tempered by skepticism.

But this is not the problem to which I wish to call attention. My difficulty is the reverse of this: Why do people go on believing in *individual instances* of (let us say) witchcraft when in general they know that witchcraft is not quite what it seems? If everybody is consciously aware that witchcraft is really a flag of convenience for the powerful tides of jealousy and aggression that well up from the unconscious, why not fly the true colors? Many anthropologists offer an answer, one that I consider partial, misleading, and con-trary to the ethnographic facts.[36] This explanation maintains that witchcraft acts as a surrogate for envy and spite in contexts where the open acknowledgment of these emotions cannot possibly be contemplated. So, it is held, witchcraft conceals and mystifies hatred. But how can it possibly do this, if everyone knows that it is hatred? Are the Zande and other peoples with comparable beliefs so benighted that they are exempt from even the most elementary Freudian principles about the relationship between conscious and unconscious affect? Of course not; but perhaps we can now identify our situation more precisely. Surely it is analogous to that fre-quently encountered in modern psychiatry, where, with the wide diffusion of Freud's teaching and of popular psychodynamic con-cepts among the laity, many patients not only possess insight into their own problems but are as fully versed in the technical jargon as their therapists. Or, to put it in a more ancient formulation: The Devil knows well how to quote Scripture for his own purposes. Such cases are, of course, notoriously difficult to treat. Can we then say that here again faith is tempered by skepticism? Or would it be better to say that skepticism is tempered by faith? When, to return to our original question, does skepticism overwhelm faith com-pletely? What do people *really* believe and feel?

This remains our oldest and most refractory problem. The clas-sical example in the empiricist fieldwork tradition is Malinowski's "discovery" that his Trobriand Islanders seemed to live in sexual innocence, touchingly believing that their wives were impregnated by spirits. This, at any rate, was the official doctrine in this matrilineal society. But did the Trobriand Islanders really believe it, or was it mere dogma to which reluctant and skeptical lip service was paid in appropriate circumstances? The difficulty of answering questions of this kind, posed in this way, is clearly shown in the wide-ranging controversy provoked by Edmund Leach's stimulating resurrection of this whole issue in his Henry Myers Lecture on "Virgin Birth."[37] Further evidence can be found in the parallel argument between Evans-Pritchard and Raymond Firth[38] on the interpretation of the relationship between twins and birds postulated by the Nuer, Tikopia, and other peoples. These fairly specific examples, moreover, are part of the wider and continuing debate regarding the structure of traditional or "primitive" thought and the many attempts to specify, analyze, and compare cosmologies. The immense popularity that Lévi-Strauss's opaque disquisitions on mythology enjoy is itself an excellent measure of the topicality of the problem.

VII

Despite so much devoted and learned attention, however, the answer to our question "What do people really believe . . . ?" is still decidedly problematical.[39] In my opinion, we have scarcely advanced beyond the achievements of Evans-Pritchard's study of Zande witchcraft. And if we still have difficulty in satisfactorily exposing the beliefs of a given people, how can we possibly embark on comparative studies of different cosmologies? Progress here is often impeded by our failure to appreciate clearly what we are trying to do. We constantly seek to leap precipitately from the concrete and particular to the abstract and general. We aspire to identify and characterize a whole people's philosophy or "world view" and to say – as we so glibly do – that one culture is more or less pious (or mystical, or ritualistic, etc.) than another. Such cardboard cosmological portraits are often just as treacherous and misleading as those that seek to depict national character (see Chapter 5). We also regularly forget what, as I have tried to show, we are forced to acknowledge when we frankly consider the true sources of our information: that faith and skepticism and various degrees of reliance on mystical or nonmystical comforts are functions of situations and circumstances. A complete inventory of the explanatory beliefs (mystical and nonmystical) available in a given culture is thus meaningless unless accompanied by a minutely detailed exposition of their deployment in actual situations, sufficiently well specified to permit rigorous comparison in other cultures. The detachment of beliefs from their ambient circumstances produces gross distortion and misunderstanding. "There are no atheists in the trenches." Again, as everybody knows, but as we anthropologists too readily forget, the passage of time is another critical variable affecting explanations of the same event (as it is reevaluated) by the same actors in the same culture at different stages in the unfolding social drama that accompanies it. Thus characterizations of the patterns of causal explanations offered for an illness or misfortune must specify the time span within which they are effective. Obviously, the same symptoms may be explained in different ways according to their temporal persistence. What accounts satisfactorily for the transient appearance of a malady is unlikely to serve to explain its persistence in a chronic form, and so on.

Those who perceive the full magnitude of the task involved here tend, understandably enough, to shrink from it, and even to give up all hope of ever achieving valid comparisons in this field of study. Other, sturdier scholars, undaunted by these dangers, bravely struggle on, sometimes – as in the case of Mary Douglas[40] – at the price of trailing off into clouds of incomprehensible whimsy. It is abundantly clear that we urgently need a more discriminating and rigorous analytical apparatus to collect and codify case histories exhibiting the actual, selective use of explanatory principles over time in clearly specified and accurately observed conditions. This is asking much. But I believe it is not impossible, and I cite as an example Gilbert Lewis's pioneering ethnomedical study of the Gnau people of the western Sepik region of New Guinea.[41] In this detailed and fully circumstantial account of the recognition of, and response to, sickness, we find precisely the kind and range of information that is essential if we are to achieve valid comparative studies of what people really think and feel. If other anthropologists were to follow this exacting example we would soon have a useful body of evidence; we could control the relevant variables and successfully compare like with like to discover the real cultural variations in response to affliction. From this starting point we could move on to a wider, objectively based comparative cosmology resting not on impressionistic summaries or "condensations" but on rigorously controlled point-by-point comparisons. I do not claim that the arguments deployed in subsequent chapters always meet these requirements, but I hope that they at least point in this direction.

2

Possession cults in context

I

Anthropologists, no less than the people they study, are much given
to the elaboration of those traditions by which men everywhere
seek to justify their current interests and activities in terms of some
mystically hallowed past. Malinowski himself was among the first
to explore the sociological implications of such "mythological
charters," as he called them. My own "charter," in this chapter, is
brief. My first point is that it seems to me, as to some of my colleagues, that many of the present impasses in our subject, which
result from a too rigid adherence to the teleological mystique of
status quo maintenance of Radcliffe-Brown (and his "structural
Marxist" perpetuators), may be resolved by taking a view of the
working of social institutions that owes more to Malinowski and
that is essentially flexible, adaptive, and utilitarian. This is the sort
of functionalism I hope to deploy here. Second, my subject matter
concerns religion and sex, topics that certainly engaged the serious
attention of Malinowski and led to the production of some of his
most inspired and most popular works. Spirit-possession, or at least
those aspects with which I shall be concerned here, embodies both
themes. I would only add that, from the tendentious aridity of current kinship controversy and the mechanical, if lofty, metaphysic of
Lévi-Strauss, this is a subject to which I turn with a distinct sense
of relief. At least the phenomena that we shall examine here have
some discernible relation to empirical reality.

Spirit-possession, from one point of view the root of mysticism,
is, one need scarcely be reminded, a vast subject. As well as the
familiars of a host of less well-known and anonymous shamans, it
embraces within a single frame of reference such well-established

figures as the Holy Ghost and "Katie King," the controversial materialization produced by the famous English medium Florence Cook and investigated and vouched for by no lesser a person than Sir William Crookes, president of the Royal Society from 1913 to 1915. Lest this conjunction seem unduly forced, let me add that for some theological writers, and not least for the Reverend J. D. Pearce-Higgins, a prominent member of the Churches' Fellowship for Psychical Study, Katie King's activities have been seen as providing corroborative evidence for scientific belief in the Resurrection of Jesus Christ (Pearce-Higgins 1957: 38).

Our topic includes such other spectacular features as dervish dancing, fire walking, sword eating, and transvestism – to say nothing of such arcane phenomena as "automatic writing." In the realm of ideas and emotions, we are at once confronted by such contradictory themes as innovative inspiration and conservative resignation expressed in catharsis; by aggressive messianic cults and by established religions based on the conservative cult of a supreme spiritual deity.

Spirit-possession thus occupies a central position in comparative religion and theology, in religious phenomenology, in the sociology of religion, and in psychology. With such a vast canvas, I can scarcely hope in a short space to do more than daub a rough outline of my subject. Certainly I cannot do anything like justice to its formidable literature.[1] I shall, however, try to draw attention to certain neglected aspects of the subject that seem to me of crucial importance in appreciating its sociological significance. These concern what in medical parlance would be called the epidemiology of possession, by which in this context I mean the examination of the categories of persons who are most readily prone to possession in different societies. This, I hope to show, is sociologically an illuminating approach and an almost completely novel one, strange though that claim may sound. The majority of writers on spirit-possession, as even a cursory glance at the literature will reveal, have been fascinated by the richly dramatic aspects of possession, enthralled by the more bizarre and exotic shamanistic exercises, and absorbed in controversies concerning the truth or falsity of trance states. In short, their main interest has been in everything pertaining to spirit-possession that, in the idiom of one of the Malinowski Lectures (Beattie 1966), could be termed "expressive."

Such sociological analysis as has been offered has focused primarily on the social roles and statuses of the chronically possessed – whether these be identified as mediums, shamans, or prophets. This position is neatly summed up in Mircea Eliade's book *Le chamanisme* (1951), which is still the standard compendium on the subject. Eliade writes of what he considers the sociologist's proper concern with spirit-possession as follows: "The sociologist is preoccupied with the social functions of the shaman, of the priest, of the magician: He will study the origin of mystical prestige, its role in the articulation of society, the relations between religious chiefs and political chiefs" (Eliade 1951: 8, my translation).

Eliade himself is primarily interested in the metaphysical implications of shamanism as a technique for the attainment of ecstasy in the course of which the shaman makes mystical voyages to heaven and mystical descents to hell. In its "true sense" all this is bound up with the cult of a supreme celestial being. Thus spirit-possession is not for Eliade an essential or intrinsic element but one that is incidental to the shaman's ecstatic mystical flights and his communion with supreme celestial beings.

This conclusion seems to me highly debatable. But whatever may be thought of it, Eliade's program for sociology represents a fair statement of what social anthropologists and others have written on spirit-possession in the past. This concentration of interest on the social roles performed only by those who through regularly recurrent possession and dramatic rituals function as mediums or shamans stands in sharp contrast to the prevailing emphasis in anthropological studies of magic, witchcraft, and sorcery. There the trend established by the pioneering works of Evans-Pritchard (1937), Kluckhohn (1944), and Marwick (1952) has been to examine in detail the social nexus in which jealousies, enmities, and frustrations between rivals are transmuted into accusations of witchcraft and sorcery. The ritual and magical acts of witch doctors and sorcerers receive due attention but do not dominate the stage to the exclusion of the relevant social tensions, which must figure prominently in any satisfactory epidemiological approach, and which have been so sadly neglected in most studies of spirit-possession.

This striking difference in analytical emphasis results partly, no doubt, from the dramatic aspects of spirit-possession that so readily seize the attention of the investigator and deflect interest away from

any detailed examination of the categories of persons most prone
to be selected as mediums by spirits. After all, despite their attitudes
toward witchcraft and sorcery, many anthropologists seem to believe
in spirit-possession, or at least in some of the powers attributed to
those possessed by spirits.[2] Thus much of the literature is taken up,
as I have said, with discussion of the psychological status of trance
states and the extent to which shamanistic healing rites possess genuine therapeutic value. Even atheists often believe in extrasensory
perception. Recent anthropological writing on witchcraft shows no
such preoccupation: there, all is delusion and fantasy.

Such considerations go far, I think, toward explaining this distinct difference of emphasis in anthropological studies in the two
fields. But whether they do or not, what I shall now try to demonstrate is that the sort of sociological approach that is now taken for
granted in the analysis of witchcraft and sorcery is equally revealing
when applied to spirit-possession. This approach has the additional
merit of bringing what has too often been regarded as an esoteric
oddity squarely into the larger field of the sociological study of mystical phenomena and of religion in general.

II

Little attention, I have asserted, has so far been paid to the question
of what categories of persons most frequently succumb to spirit-
possession and figure most prominently in possession cults. Nevertheless, the literature is studded with references to the frequent
prominence of women in these cults; and some explicit attempts
have been made to explain, or at least to comment on, this sexual
bias on the part of spirits. Thus W. G. Ivens notes that among the
Melanesians of the southeast Solomon Islands, although women
are rigorously excluded from the "greater" religious ceremonies,
they have a share in the offering of the first fruits, and on other
occasions become possessed and may divine and intercede for the
sick (Ivens 1927: 472). Similarly, Hogbin notes how in Polynesia
women are frequently the mediums consulted for those diseases
ascribed to possession by the spirits of the ancestors, this involving
a combination of patrilineal and matrilineal ancestral power (Hogbin 1934: 144ff.) With more detail and sophistication, Fortune shows
how among the Manus of New Guinea, while women are, as he
puts it, "spiritually disenfranchised in the [paternal] Sir Ghost cult,

they are spiritually enfranchised in the *tandritanitani* cults" (Fortune 1935: 95). This statement refers to the mystical power of cursing and blessing, the ability to control the sex of children, and family planning – all vested in the matrilineal line. Moreover, while the morally significant patrilineal ghost cult is controlled by men, it is women who consecrate male diviners and practice as mediums. Here there is a complicated interplay between men's and women's roles that corresponds, to some extent, to the character of the descent system in Manus, any further discussion of which would take us outside the scope of the present argument.

In the same vein, A. J. A. Elliott in his detailed study of Chinese spirit-possession cults in Singapore notes how, as among the Manus, women are the principal mediums in the raising of the souls of the dead, though not necessarily in the wider practice of spirit mediumship. Yet although in the wider cult it is not only women who act as mediums, it is women who provide the main clientele (Eliott 1955: 71, 134ff.). And in Africa, among the matrilineal Luvale of western Zambia, C. M. N. White has shown the prominent part played by women as the victims of illnesses attributed to possession by their matrilineal ancestors (White 1961: 48ff.).[3]

Again, in that magnificent record of the life of an old Hausa woman, Baba of Karo, the very marked absorption of women in the cult of *bori* spirits elicits the comment from Mary Smith that in this male-dominated Muslim society the "inability of the Hausa women to participate adequately in the ceremonial and public life of Islam leaves a gap which is filled by the spirit-possession cult" (Mary Smith 1954: 271).

These and similar comments by many other observers of such cults, which it would be tedious to cite further at this point, typify the line of interpretation that views the prominent role of women in spirit-possession as a compensation for their exclusion and lack of authority in other spheres. A similar cross-sexual element is apparent in the imagery and ritual drama of possession ceremonies. For whether it is men or women who are the victims of possession – and, of course, I am not claiming that it is only women who are thus affected – the intrusive familiar is frequently of the sex opposite to that of the host. With this high incidence of the possession of men by female spirits, and of women by male spirits, it is scarcely surprising that the relationship between a medium and his or her attendant familiar should regularly be expressed in terms of marriage. Indeed, in many spirit mediumship cults, full introduction into the coterie of the chronically possessed is accompanied by marriage ceremonies and gifts that parallel those of mortal unions. Thus in the flamboyant *zar* cult in Ethiopia the new acolyte is referred to as a "bride" and is assigned two human protectors or "best men." These in ordinary marriages may assist the husband to deflower his bride, and subsequently act as her supporters in all disputes between the wife and her husband (Messing 1959: 327). In the same vein, when a medium exhibits agitated bodily movements in an ecstatic trance it is a commonplace to regard the possessed woman as having intercourse with her incubus.

This matrimonial theme is, of course, familiar to us from the Roman Catholic religious tradition, in which a nun's final vows bind her in spiritual union to the sacred bridegroom, Christ. In the rather different but equally widespread idiom of the stables, in which the relationship between a woman medium and her spirit is expressed in terms of the familiar riding its "mare," this cross-sexual imagery is equally apparent. The cross-sexual element is also evoked in the ceremonial transvestism that accompanies many possession rituals and has been taken by some earlier students of the subject, notably by Leo Sternberg (1924), as an essential and indeed definitive characteristic of the whole phenomenon.

III

I believe, however, that by adopting the epidemiological approach we can go much farther in interpreting the social implications of spirit-possession. Let me start, in the manner of Malinowski, with a brief exposition of my own Somali field material.[4] The Somali pastoral nomads of northeast Africa are a patrilineal Muslim people. Witchcraft and sorcery, as these phenomena are usually defined, do not figure prominently in Somali ideas of causation. Their main religious life is concerned with the cult of Allah, whom they approach through the mediation of the Prophet Mohammed and a host of more immediate lineage ancestors and other men of real or imputed piety who, as in Roman Catholicism, play a vital role as mediating saints. This public cult is almost exclusively dominated by men, who hold all the main positions of religious authority and prestige. Women in religion are merely passive agents and, as in many other

Muslim countries, are excluded from the mosques. More generally, women are regarded as weak, submissive creatures, despite the demanding nature of their nomadic life, particularly the arduous herding of flocks of sheep, goats, and the draft camels that carry their tents and effects. Milch camels, by contrast, are the concern of men; and although women are disadvantageously placed in the inheritance of all forms of property, they are especially excluded from ownership of the camels, which form the joint stock-wealth of groups and represent the standard unit of wealth.

In this male-dominated and highly puritanical culture, spirit-possession, which is regarded as one cause among others of a wide range of illnesses and diseases (ranging from slight malaise to acute organic illness) occurs in four fairly well-defined contexts. The first of those concerns cases of frustrated love or passion and involves emotions that, particularly on the part of men, are not traditionally recognized or overtly acknowledged. If a girl who has been jilted by a boy she loved and who promised privately to marry her exhibits symptoms of extreme lassitude, withdrawal, or even more distinct physical symptoms of illness, her condition is attributed to possession by the object of her affections. Here, as in all other cases in Somaliland, this possession is described most generally by a term that means literally "entering."

This interpretation of the disappointed girl's condition is consistent with the traditional sex morality, from which the concept of romantic attachment is, as I have said, excluded. Only within the last generation has this rigid attitude apparently begun to change; and today the explicit recognition and acceptance of romantic love are a common theme in Somali poetry and popular songs. Reflecting these enlightened views, young Western-educated Somalis today describe such cases as a kind of love sickness. The traditional view, on the other hand, is much more in keeping with that exhibited by seventeenth-century French Catholic ecclesiastics in their treatment of the hysterical Sister Jeanne des Anges, prioress of the convent school of Loudon, and her frustrated infatuation for the notoriously amorous Canon Urbain Grandier. As those who have read Aldous Huxley's lively evocation in *The Devils of Loudon* (1952) will recall, this poor nun's condition was attributed to possession by malevolent spirits, and Grandier was held responsible. He was convicted of witchcraft and burned at the stake in 1634.

In Somalia these matters are dealt with less harshly, and no legal action can be taken against the man involved. But it is not only men who are the agents or women the victims in this type of affliction. A youth, forced by the overriding control of his elder kinsman to renounce the girl of his own choosing and impelled to marry another, may, if he evinces similar symptoms of malaise or illness, be regarded as possessed by the true object of his affections.

My own interpretation is virtually the same as that offered by young educated Somalis themselves. In the case of the jilted girl, no other institutionalized means is available to express her outraged feelings. For it is only where a formal engagement has been contracted with the consent of the two parties of kin that a suit can be lodged for breach of promise. Her private emotions and feelings are of little concern in a jural world dominated by men. Illness and the associated care and attention offer her some comfort. In the case of the frustrated youth, the assimilation of his plight into an illness – for which he cannot in Somali theory be held responsible – similarly enables him to draw attention to his unhappiness without openly revealing the unmentionable and totally unmanly emotional attachment of a man to a woman.[5]

While these are both examples of cross-sexual possession of one person by another, the underlying circumstances are those of deprivation, in which no other jurally acceptable and institutionalized means exists to enable the injured party to seek redress. This sort of direct, person-to-person possession has close analogies with the malevolent power of the evil eye attributed to forlorn, neglected old women, to beggars, and to the poor in general. Of the treatment administered to the possessed patient in these cases I shall say here only that, as with Sister Jeanne des Anges, the invading spirit is exorcised by a cleric,[6] in this case a Muslim man of religion.[7]

In the other three contexts of Somali spirit-possession to which I wish to draw attention, the possession illness – with parallel symptoms, real or imagined, ranging from mild hysteria or depression to actual organic injury – is attributed to the "entering" not of a person but of a nature sprite. Here I refer to those anthropomorphic *jinns* that in Somalia, as in other Muslim lands, are held to lurk in every dark and empty corner, poised and ready to strike capriciously and without warning at the unwary passerby. These malevolent sprites are said to be consumed by envy and greed and to be particularly covetous of luxurious clothing, finery, perfume, and dainty goods. They are known generally as *sar* (Ethiopian *zar*), a word that describes both the sprites themselves and the symptoms attributed to them; the afflicted victim is described as having been "entered," "seized," or "possessed" by the *sar*.

These are the agencies to which responsibility is attributed for the bouts of hysteria to which young camel herdsmen are some-times prone. The circumstances are as follows. The camels, as I have said, are herded by the men, and more specifically by boys and young unmarried youths. In the charge of these young men, the camels form a herding unit separate from the flocks of sheep and goats that are attached to the nomadic hamlets consisting of women, married men, and young children. The latter herding unit has a much more tightly circumscribed cycle of movement than that fol-lowed by the free-ranging camels, which even in the driest seasons can go without water for up to twenty days and graze far from any permanent well. Thus the camels and their young attendants live a secluded life of their own, often stationing themselves hundreds of miles from the home hamlet and their womenfolk. In the dry sea-sons, the herdsmen move monotonously back and forth between the pastures and the wells, according to a strict regime dictated by the watering needs of their stock. By any standards their dry-season lot is especially hard and demanding. Constantly harassed by fear of attack from enemy raiders and marauding animals, and fre-quently short of food and water, they are also deprived of the opportunity to meet and chat with the girls of the hamlets. With no regular means of cooking, their diet consists mainly of the milk of the camels in their care; often they are as famished and exhausted as their stock.

In the wet seasons, when the water requirements of sheep and goats, on the one hand, and of camels, on the other, are more evenly balanced, this dreary picture radically changes. The two herding units now move closer together, and the young camel herdsmen emerge from their dry-season seclusion and privation to the com-fort and excitement of camp life. It is on their return to this other, welcoming world, with its prospect of meeting girls of marriageable age, that young herdsmen sometimes develop symptoms of hys-teria. This is attributed to possession by *sar* sprites and regarded as a mild and usually temporary form of madness; it is not taken very seriously. The remedy is provided by the mounting of a dance called "beating the *sar,*" in which it is essential that girls should participate if the smitten youths are "to recover their senses." The accompanying songs, sung by the boys, often have an implicit sexual content, and the expression "beating the *sar*" is, in modern urban slang at least, a synonym for sexual intercourse. In this traditional pastoral setting, however, the youths must content themselves with catharsis and sublimation. There is no open license on these occasions, and the virginity of girls is carefully guarded until they marry. Today, however, the situation seems to be changing, even in the interior. This type of "possession," I am told, is now often feigned and used by youths as a means of pointing the direction of their affections toward a particular girl, who is thus drawn into the dance. All I wish to emphasize here, however, is the element of deprivation and frustration present in the lives of these young bachelor herdsmen, and its traditional outlet in this institutionalized form of possession.[8]

This brings us to the third context of Somali possession, where we touch on a phenomenon that I believe has the widest significance and correspondences elsewhere. The victim of the malevolent *sar*'s attentions is in this case usually a woman, most often a married woman. The stock epidemiological situation is that of the hard-pressed wife struggling to survive and feed her children in the harsh environment, and liable to some degree of neglect, real or imagined, on the part of her husband. Subjected to frequent, sudden, and even prolonged absences by her husband as he pursues his manly pastoral interests and affairs, to the jealousies and tensions of polygyny here not ventilated in accusations of sorcery or witchcraft, and always menaced by the precariousness of marriage in a society where divorce is frequent and particularly easily obtained by men, the Somali married woman's lot offers little stability or security. It is scarcely surprising, therefore, that many women's ailments, whether accompanied by definite physical symptoms or not, should be readily interpreted by them as possession by *sar* spirits demanding luxurious clothes, perfume, and delicate foods from their menfolk. It is only when these costly demands are met, and when all the other expenses involved in the mounting of a cathartic dance ("beating the *sar*"), directed by an expert female shaman, are paid, that the symptoms can be expected to disappear. Even then, relief from the affliction may be only temporary.

Without instancing all the evidence I have collected on such cases, let me simply record that in several of them the onset of this sprite affliction coincided with a husband's opening moves to marry an additional spouse, and that in every example known to me some grudge against her spouse was borne by the woman concerned. It scarcely requires the sophisticated forensic techniques of modern anthropology to discover what is involved here; and, very properly, Somali men draw their own conclusions. What the wives call *sar* possession, their husbands call malingering, and they interpret this affliction as yet another of the deceitful tricks employed by women against men. Men support this charge by alleging that the incidence of the disease is much higher among the wives of the wealthy than among those of the poor. This insinuation women in their turn counter with the sophistry that there are some *sar* sprites that attack the wealthy and others that molest the poor. Despite this sociological view of the situation, men's attitudes are in fact ambivalent: They believe in the existence of these *sar* sprites, but with true Somali pragmatism they become skeptical when their own womenfolk and their own pockets are affected.

Depending on the marital circumstances and the value placed on the wife affected, the usual reaction is for the husband to accept reluctantly one or two bouts of this kind. But if the affliction becomes chronic, and the wife becomes a more or less regular member of a circle of *sar* devotees, save in exceptional circumstances the husband's patience soon wears thin. If a good thrashing will not do the trick, there is always the threat of divorce; and unless the woman herself desires this (as she may), or is actually psychiatrically ill and cannot control her symptoms, this seems usually to work.

Leaving aside the wider implications of membership in a regular association of female *sar* devotees, the point I want to stress here is that in general this characteristically woman's affliction operates among the Somali as a limited deterrent against the abuses of neglect and deprivation in a conjugal relationship heavily biased in favor of men. In a society that offers them little domestic security and very inadequately protects them otherwise from the pressures and demands of men, women may thus resort to spirit-possession, I am arguing, as a means both of obliquely airing their grievances and of gaining some satisfaction. This way of looking at the phenomenon immediately ranks it with such other modes of mystical retaliation as witchcraft and sorcery practiced in societies with other cultural traditions and cosmologies.

This may seem a big jump. But when the social nexus is fully considered the analogy is, I think, justified, and it may seem more acceptable when it is remembered that in many societies witches in fact perform their dark acts by means of spirit familiars. Thus in many cases there is not only a functional parallel between the effects of spirit-possession and those of witchcraft but also an ideological one. I recognize, of course, that it is not the guilty husband but the aggrieved wife who in the Somali case is mystically afflicted. But, as I shall try to show, this difference between an oblique use of mystical power with, in effect, a self-inflicted injury and the more direct line of attack in witchcraft and sorcery is not so critical as might at first appear.

Finally, I mention briefly the last context of Somali possession affliction. This primarily concerns adult men, and not so much a definable social category of men but, rather, psychologically disturbed individuals who, for one reason or another, experience particular difficulties in bearing the pressures and burdens of their society. Just as men are regarded as of the dominant sex and consequently less vulnerable than women, the spirits possessing these unfortunate individuals are considered to be particularly deadly. Again, since men hold the dominant role in the cult of Islam, it is appropriate that the powers involved here should be regarded not merely as especially dangerous but also as especially religious. They are in fact the spiritual analogues of human Muslim clerics, so I call them "clerical sprites." These clerical sprites, I hasten to add, are not a unique Somali aberration but, on the contrary, belong to a category of spirits well known in other Muslim countries and for the existence of which there is, moreover, scriptural warrant in the Koran.[9]

These four contexts of Somali spirit-possession are connected by the common themes of confinement and frustration, which occur in different ways in all of them. This is perhaps most evident in the case of the aggrieved wives, where, to adopt current phraseology, spirits enter the "sex-war." Now the *sar* culture-complex with this emphasis is not confined to the Somali alone. It exists also in Ethio-

pia (as *zar*), where it reaches its greatest shamanistic elaboration
and where it seems to have originated (Cerulli 1923: 2); and it has
spread not only into Somalia but also into the northern Sudan, Egypt,
and even the sacred city of Mecca itself (Hurgronje 1931).

Its psychological and dramatic aspects in Ethiopia have been
described and analyzed most subtly by the brilliant French surrealist poet and ethnographer Michel Leiris (1958). Further light has
been shed on its social significance in that country by the work of
an American anthropologist, Simon Messing (1958; 1959). Messing records how wives have used the cult in Somali fashion to extort
economic sacrifices from their husbands, threatening a relapse when
their demands are ignored. Much the same appears to happen in
Egypt; and in Cairo, where the cult is prevalent, a particular shop
specializes in the sale of the appropriate costumes and other regalia
used in the *zar* ceremonies by the female "brides" of the spirits
(Kriss and Kriss-Heinrich 1962). This theme is even more explicitly
displayed in the suburbs of Khartoum. A recent account reports
that here *zar* spirits possessing wives not only demand gifts, including in one case gold teeth, but may also roundly upbraid the latters'
husbands in terms that would not be tolerated in other circumstances (Barclay 1964: 198; see also Constantinides 1977).

IV

These "sex-war" aspects are by no means restricted to the *zar*-com-
plex but occur widely in spirit-possession in a variety of societies
and places. I do not pretend to have made an exhaustive search of
the literature, but I record a few scattered examples. In African
ethnography one of the earliest and best descriptions comes from
Lindblom's study of the Akamba of east Africa (Lindblom 1920:
229–40). Here a sharp distinction is drawn between the ancestral
spirits, which uphold morality and represent the ongoing interests
of their descendants, and other capricious spirits. These latter are
typically of neighboring tribes – Masai, Galla, and Wanyika – and
include Europeans. They are not worshiped but frequently plague
Kamba women, who must then be exorcised. As with possession
elsewhere, these afflicted women speak "in tongues" in an obscure
jargon; but despite the problems of communication, their demands
are quite clear. They seek gifts and attention from their menfolk,
usually husbands, each spirit asking for things appropriate to its

provenance. Thus Swahili spirits demand embroidered Arab hats; and European spirits, articles of European origin. Women may make use of the cult to force their husbands to buy clothing for them. In a poignant little case history, Lindblom records how a woman with a longing for meat could only gain her husband's consent to the killing of an animal by resort to a possession bout in which her cravings were voiced by the invading spirit. Unfortunately, however, she made the mistake, once her desires were satisfied, of vaunting her successful deceit too openly; she was sent back to her father by her outraged spouse.

Parallel instances are reported from Tanzania, where an affliction, popularly called "devil's disease" in Swahili, is apt to plague women. Again, the possessing spirit, which manifests its presence by hysterical and other symptoms, demands gifts, some of which reflect its provenance. Treatment is a fairly lengthy business, involving not only the usual costly cathartic dances but also the presence for some time of the therapist within the afflicted woman's family. In this enlightened form of therapy, the sick woman is thus made to feel the center of attention; her husband may even be constrained to modify his behavior toward her (Koritschoner 1936). Again from east Africa, in an extremely interesting study of the Taita of Kenya, Grace Harris (1957) describes a similar women's possession affliction, by spirits other than those of the main, morally endowed, male-dominated cult, that functions in a similar manner to exert pressure on men. Here an important element, present in many of the cathartic rites associated with these spirit afflictions, is the assumption by women of male postures and dress.

Analogous phenomena have been described by several observers among the BaThonga (Junod 1922) and Zulu (Krige 1936: 307; Gluckman 1954) of South Africa; in the case of the Zulu, psychological studies are also available (Lee 1950 and 1969; Loudon 1959). Among Junod's Thonga, women were traditionally afflicted by Zulu and other foreign spirits, and the Zulu women in turn by Thonga devils. In both cases there is the familiar pattern of hysterical and other manifestations, as well as requests for gifts and for the mounting of the cathartic dance paid for by the husband. Among the Zulu today, however, this affliction – known locally as "Bantu disease" and diagnosed by Lee as a form of conversion hysteria – most commonly involves possession by Indian spirits and by the *tokoloshe,* obscene little sprites with thickset bodies and huge penises. All this readily lends itself to straightforward Freudian interpretation, and Lee records cures effected on this basis. My interest here is in the institutionalized role of this Zulu possession cult in the sex-war. In this connection I note in passing Loudon's intriguing observation that the rise of these typically feminine disorders seems to have coincided with the decline of the traditional agricultural fertility rituals in which women exchanged their habitual role of submission for one of dominance. These now-extinct rituals are among those referred to by Gluckman in his Frazer Lecture *Rituals of Rebellion in South-east Africa* (1952).

We turn now to west Africa, where elements similar to those we have been discussing may, I believe, be found in the Songhay cult of *holey* sprites and in the Hausa *bori* cult. For the Songhay, I admit, the evidence is not entirely clear. Jean Rouch (1960: 178ff.) records that possession by these *holey* spirits in this Islamized society is more frequently invoked as an explanation of illness in women than in men, although as in many of the other cases we have been considering, men of low status may also be afflicted. Again, there is a whole family of these sprites, some associated with neighboring peoples (such as the Hausa and Tuareg) and others with animals. A modern addition to this spirit host is that of European sprites, who increasingly appear unbidden at the seances in which women play so important a part. Here there is a well-organized establishment of societies of mediums and shamans, in which the low-caste Sorko fisherfolk play a crucial role, along with the usual dances, gifts, and offerings. There is no explicit indication, however, that the cult offers women the direct means of exerting the pressure on their menfolk that we have discovered elsewhere. Further research, I suggest, may well reveal that it does.

The Hausa *bori* cult, which like that of *zar* has spread northward into north Africa, is a similar though more elaborate affair.[10] Here there is a great pantheon of some two hundred individually named sprites, related in various ways among themselves in a manner reminiscent of the gods of ancient Greece. These *bori,* according to Tremearne (1913), range in descending order of importance from the mighty "king of the *jinns*" (*Sarkin'Aljan*) to a small cluster of sprites known familiarly as the "little spots," which despite their innocent-sounding name are held to be responsible not only for a number of minor ailments but also for smallpox. This *bori* pantheon is thus not merely a census of spiritual forces but equally a medical dictionary, each sprite being connected with a group of symptoms (some of which overlap). Both among the Muslim Hausa in west Africa proper and in its northern extension in Tunisia, Tripolitania, and Egypt, this cult is again predominantly one of women, who are the regular devotees in shamanistic exercises designed to exorcise the grounds of their ailments.

But I believe that we can go farther and bring some elements of this elaborate cult within our particular purview. A search of the scattered literature is not very rewarding; the most suggestive clues are that the evil eye is believed to operate through the agency of *bori* sprites (Tremearne 1914: 179) and that a despised and neglected wife is known as a *bora*, a term that Tremearne (1914: 395) connects with *bori*. I do not know whether this is valid etymology or not. But a more recent observer records that in practice the *bori* cult has two main aspects – one inside the Hausa compound and the other outside.[11] Of these, the latter and wider cult has hitherto received more attention from anthropologists. In the internal domestic cult, which has been neglected, *bori* possession, involving only certain selected spirits of the total pantheon, appears to be used especially by junior co-wives against their senior colleagues and particularly against their husbands; it thus figures prominently in disputes within the polygynous family. Here, as in the other cases we have examined, wives possessed by *bori* exact gifts and economic sacrifices from their husbands and in this fashion press their claims for attention.

Finally, a diligent search of the literature will, I think, yield examples outside Africa of the particular type of mystical sanction we have been discussing. Certainly, as I pointed out earlier, women and persons of other subject categories figure prominently in many spirit cults elsewhere in the world, and not least in our own shamanistic tradition, where the sexual element is certainly by no means absent. One well-established non-African phenomenon that seems to support this argument is found among the polar Eskimos and other Siberian peoples and is usually known as "Arctic hysteria." This is a hysterical affliction mainly affecting women and particularly prevalent during the harsh winter months in northern Greenland. Gussow (1960), who interprets this condition in Freudian terms, considers the hysterical flights to which those affected are prone as unconscious seductive maneuvers and invitations to male pursuit. They are, he argues, the refuge of those women who in hardship and crisis seek loving reassurance. Stripped of its Freudian cadences, this interpretation suggests my own line of analysis. It is, moreover, particularly significant in this connection that this hysterical condition, which is generally attributed to spirit-possession, plays a vital part in the selection, training, and ritual performances of Siberian shamans – who are frequently women (Czaplicka 1914: 169ff., 309–25).[12] More recent studies (e.g., Basilov 1981) argue that over the last few decades, with increasing secularization in the Soviet Union, shamanism has been marginalized and has become almost exclusively the province of women.

V

It must now be clear, I think, that we are concerned here with a widespread use of spirit-possession, by means of which women and other depressed categories exert mystical pressures on their superiors in circumstances of deprivation and frustration when few other sanctions are available to them. Of course, spirit-possession is only one possible mystical mode, and one that operates obliquely in the sense that it is the aggrieved party who submits to the affliction rather than seeking to inflict illness on the real source of injury and deprivation. Witchcraft and sorcery are from this point of view other, more direct processes of retaliation and attack; and I do not attempt to determine why in certain societies one mode is favored rather than another – or indeed why in some cases both are found. It may be worth noting, however, that one specific characteristic of spirit-possession is that, unlike at least some forms of witchcraft and sorcery, it appears usually to offer an explanation only of illness. It does not generally explain external misfortunes, at least not directly, and this seems to follow logically from the specific nature of possession as an invasion of the person.

Whether or not this will turn out to be a valid and significant distinction, there are important analogies between the two types of mystical sanction – spirit-possession, and witchcraft and sorcery – to which I have already referred and would like now to press further. It seems to me that in Nadel's analysis of Nupe witchcraft, for instance, we find a kind of witchcraft converse to the enlistment by women of spirits in the "sex-war" that has been our main theme so far. For here, through their enterprise in trade and commerce, which often makes their husbands financially indebted to them, it is women who get out of hand and cannot be brought to heel except by accusing them of being witches (Nadel 1952). One further point in this regard seems worth making. The best anthropological analysts of witchcraft and sorcery strongly emphasize the nexus of conflict between the bewitched or ensorceled victim and the witch or sorcerer. They tend to forget, however, that in pointing the finger of accusation at the witch or sorcerer, the victim also draws attention to himself (or herself). This, I suggest, has the effect not merely of marshaling public opinion behind the victim in the manner of the typical witch hunt but also of making the victim the center of special care and consideration. This, at least, seems to be a common effect of the whole process, one that has been singularly neglected in witchcraft analysis. (These issues are pursued further in Chapter 3.)

In so far emphasizing the sanction and control aspect of the use of spirit-possession by women against men, I am not forgetting that other line of interpretation which sees in such phenomena the assertion of the interdependence of the sexes and the conservation of the existing pattern of relations between them. This is the main emphasis of Gluckman's *Rituals of Rebellion,* which reflects the traditional structural approach of Radcliffe-Brown. Thus for Gluckman such conflicts *really* represent disguised conservation and stability. This is also the main focus in Grace Harris's interpretation of the Taita women's possession cults to which I referred earlier. She, like Gluckman, in the latter's terminology sees depressed women not as suffragettes but as passive subjects, bravely shouldering their man-imposed burdens and only periodically reacting against them in a cathartic ritual acceptance of the established order. In a similar vein, Werbner (1964) has offered an elaborate analysis of Kalanga Shona women's spirit-possession. Although he does show how women use their powers to generate pressures, Werbner argues (if I have understood him correctly) that this in the end is to the profit of men. Here, however, the cult in question is much more central to the upholding of the traditional tribal morality than are the peripheral cults from which I have drawn my conclusions about the special role of women's possession.

In any case, I believe that the material I have so far presented on these peripheral cults supports my emphasis which is less on the conservative, status quo maintaining aspects than on the dynamic role of the mystical sanctions in the war between the sexes. In short, my argument is that if in these traditionally male-dominated societies women are not always actually feminists, they can readily become so when the circumstances are appropriate. I now refer for supporting evidence to a penetrating study by Elizabeth Colson (1969) of the Tonga of Zambia. By contrasting the conservative, traditionalist, valley Tonga with their more sophisticated and acculturated plateau countrymen, and using historical evidence, Colson's material reveals what really is at stake in these women's deprivation cults.

Among the plateau Tonga, who have been increasingly involved in the modern market economy of Zambia since the 1930s, and who have local opportunities for earning cash wages that do not require their menfolk to work extensively as absent migrant laborers, there has been a virtually parallel acculturation of men and women. Moreover, the traditional pattern of relations between the sexes is one of equality rather than inequality (Colson 1958: 137). Thus, like men, whether unmarried or married, women participate freely in social activities and are not strongly hedged about with mystical or other constraints. In this situation possession by peripheral *masabe* spirits is today rare, and in so far as it exists affects men and women equally.

Among the valley Tonga the situation is altogether different. Here men have long participated through labor migration in the wider European-oriented world, while women have remained at home, fascinated by the town delights and mysteries but excluded from them. It is these secluded and excluded wives who are regularly subject to possession by spirits, which today characteristically demand gifts that these women associate with their alluring urban counterparts – gay cloths, luxury foods, or (one of the commonest demands of the spirits) or soap. This demand for soap reflects a growing male sophistication, a repugnance for the traditional oil and ochre cosmetics applied by valley women, a preference for freshly bathed and fragrantly scented partners. It is in this cosmetic idiom that, through their possessing spirits, these rural women today call attention to their exclusion and neglect and seek to overcome it. In the past, their spirits desired men's garments and possessions.

Thus it is that these women's deprivation cults mirror the chang-

ing interests and desires of those who succumb to possession. These
ambitions and longings are no longer static, if they ever truly were,
and thus cannot be completely contained or explained in the repetitive idiom of ritual rebellion. Equally, the changing character and
imagery of the possessing spirits mirrors changing circumstances.
To the foreign tribal and animal sprites everywhere so prominent
in these traditional spirit pantheons are now added, while they are
still novel and mysterious, such other alien powers as those manifest in airplanes and trains. Much the same occurs with spiritual
forces of Christian mission origin, which are equally readily assimilated into these peripheral women's cults. With these new accretions, reflecting new contacts and new experiences, some of the old
spirits disappear.

Thus, contrasting the record of these cults among the valley Tonga
with the position on the plateau, it is clear how in the former case
much of the traditional inequality between the sexes continues and
so the cults continue, with modifications in the cast of invading
spirits corresponding to changing experience of the world. For the
plateau Tonga, with their more liberal treatment of women, such
possession of this type as exists continues to affect men and women
equally. This makes sense only if we acknowledge the at least
potential dynamism which I have stressed in these cults.[13]

Now let us take up a different but related theme. I have several
times called attention to the fact that the cults with which we are
mainly concerned here are peripheral in the sense that they do not
embody the main moral code of the societies in which they occur.
Thus, it seems more than merely semantically appropriate that many
of the spirits that figure in them should represent and reflect peripheral contact with foreign peoples and tangential exposure to novel
experiences. But of much greater relevance to my argument is their
special connection with women. For whether or not they may be
regarded as pawns in the marriage alliance games that Levi-Strauss's
men play, there is no doubt that in a great many societies, and
perhaps most, women are in fact *treated* as peripheral creatures.

This I hasten to add is not some special feature limited to patrilineal societies: the valley Tonga are not patrilineal, nor are many
of the examples to which I have referred. Here, I may perhaps be
permitted to interpolate, we have again a demonstration of the
unimportance, from many points of view, of these traditional descent

categories with which anthropologists have so long and so unpro-
ductively wrestled in the search for fruitful correlations with other
social phenomena. At least some anthropologists[14] now realize that
descent is a very shaky peg upon which to hang securely many
important social phenomena: That great encrusted heart of traditional anthropology is trembling, or should be.

For the peripherality of women is, irrespective of descent, a general feature of all societies where men hold a secure monopoly on
the major power positions and deny thier partners effective jural
rights. Here, of course, there is an obvious and vital contradiction,
since whatever the jural position of women, it is they who are essential to the perpetuation of life and of men. It is they who produce
and rear children, playing a major role in their early training and
education. Thus the treatment of women as peripheral creatures
flatly contradicts their fundamental biological importance and, in
social terms, clashes with their deep commitment to a particular
society and culture. (This point is elaborated in Ardener 1972.)
Hence, if it is in terms of the exclusion of women from social and
political life and their jural deprivation in relation to men that we
seek to understand their prominence in spirit-possession, we must
also recognize that these cults, expressing as they do sexual tensions, are yet allowed to exist by men. Here it seems to me possible
that this tolerance by men of the cults, and the ritual license and
blessing allowed to women more generally, may reflect a shadowy
recognition of the contradiction between the status of women and
their commitment to society. Such considerations, naturally, do not
fully explain the existence of the cults. Up to a point, as with other
mystical explanations of illness, the use of spirit-possession as a
way of classifying and treating disease implies ignorance of, disregard for, or dissatisfaction with the explanations of modern medical science. It need hardly be added that it also requires a certain
prevalence of illness.

VI

Let me conclude this, as it must seem to some, excessive concentration on female ailments by trying to draw together other strands of
the discussion into a wider schema of spirit-possession. Nadel (1946)
and many others have drawn attention not merely to the changing,
flexible, adaptive character of spirit-possession cults, which we have

seen exemplified among the Tonga, but also to their frankly innovative potential, epitomized in the "speaking with tongues" of
prophets. Let us note also that not only have we been concentrating
on peripheral cults connected with women, but that here and there
socially deprived categories of men, and maladjusted individual men,
have also slipped in. Indeed, in the *zar* cult in Ethiopia, as with the
bori and *holey* cults and others elsewhere, there is evidence of a
progressively widening spirit catchment. Not only women, but all
the rejected and despised – whether they belong to distinguishable
subordinate social categories or, as with Somali men smitten by
clerical sprites, represent individual deviants – appear increasingly
to be absorbed into such cults. Thus in Ethiopia, where in the past
women were the main devotees, ex-slaves and people of servile origin and subordinate status generally now seem to find in chronic
possession and regular membership in the cult organization a measure of security and opportunity for the enhancement of their position (Messing 1959: 331). Membership in the *zar* club itself offers
some emancipation from frustrating traditional confinements, and
one new trend toward upward mobility is also evident – the
increasingly exalted rank of the spirits that possess people of low
status.

In this connection, and especially with regard to the relief offered
to those devotees who are genuinely psychologically disturbed, I do
not wish to minimize the positive therapeutic functions seemingly
fulfilled by the regular use of cathartic and other expressive techniques in these cults.[15] Where possession is peripheral, of course,
one cannot say as Marvin Opler (1959: 112) in effect says of the
Indian peyote cult, that it is the mescaline of the masses. But even
where such cults play a subsidiary role, there is evidence that – as
well as sometimes anticipating Freud in their recognition of unconscious emotions and motivations[16] – many tribal peoples have
developed curative techniques in their shamanistic therapy that
modern psychotherapy has only recently rediscovered.

But I am afraid that I am straying from my wider schema or
spectrum of possession cults. At one end of such a spectrum lie the
phenomena that have been our main concern here. They can be
characterized as forms of hysterical possession institutionalized
mainly as a means by which women, and sometimes other subject
categories, are enabled to protect their interests and prefer their

claims and ambitions through occasional rather than chronic affliction. There is little formal elaboration of a regular shamanistic cult
as such, and the range of spirits involved may be relatively narrow.
Spirit-possession here, as we have found it among the Somali, Kamba,
Zulu, and others, has much the same effect as witchcraft and sorcery elsewhere, although it expresses tensions more obliquely.

In the next band on the spectrum, spirit-possession becomes more
the regular, stereotyped, and thoroughly institutionalized mode of
entry into a specifically shamanistic cult group, with an organized
leadership and following. Still peripheral to the main religious cult
in terms of which men's actions are evaluated and the universe
interpreted, it appeals primarily to women and to other excluded
and subordinate categories, as well as to individual deviants. Here
more than in the previous case, where the accent was primarily on
exorcism, there is a true and regular cult of spirits that may be
highly elaborate and encompass a vast pantheon of powers. This is
the situation in Singapore, in Haitian voodoo (Metraux 1959), among
the Muslim Hausa, Songhay, and the Muslim and Christian Ethiopians, to say nothing of parallel cults in classical antiquity. In these
examples it is primarily through regular membership in the cult
organization, with its prominent psychodramatic features, that
adherents gain assurance, security, and enhancement of status, even
if only vicariously. Although essentially not the bearers of the main
morality of the society in which they are found, such cults may have
great social as well as psychological importance. Here I refer to
much more than the shaman's role as fortune teller, diviner, healer,
and mediator, significant though these functions undoubtedly are.
Think, for example, of the fascinating though as yet hardly explored
social implications of the Hausa *bori* cult, with its emphasis not
only on the oldest trade of all, but also upon prosperity in trade in
general, and hence its vital mystical connection with the founding
and success of market centers, where at the salons of the richly
adorned *bori* courtesans, nobles as well as commoners vie for favor
in the highly stylized idiom of Hausa praise songs.

Such elaborate possession cults as this next shade into true prophetic movements, where the possessed mediums and shamans not
only answer recurring problems within their own cultural tradition,
but in response to new stimuli and pressures announce messianic
revelations and inaugurate spiritually inspired religions with a new

and wider appeal and a strong element of moral teaching. The precipitating circumstances and the salient characteristics of such "religions of the oppressed," as Lanternari calls them, have received a
great deal of attention both within and outside the Christian tradition.[17] Thus it is scarcely necessary to enumerate examples, beyond
pointing out that these include such embryonic and inchoate forms
as anti-witchcraft movements and cargo cults, as well as the messianic cults of Christianity and Islam. What may be of greater significance is how often, and perhaps generally, such religions stress
eschatological notions of a morally evaluative afterlife. The moral
order is sustained not merely by prosperity and happiness in this
life, but more significantly by the conferment of these rewards in
heaven.

Finally, there are those thoroughly established religions where
such a central messianic revelation of moral teaching has shrunk to
the proportions of a mere myth of creation and of the origins of
man's misery. Here, religion has been so completely assimilated into
social life, and so firmly embedded in morality, that the eschatological tradition has lost its savor. Yet such religions are still per-
meated by the notion of spirit, regularly manifest in their defense
of morality and piety through possession afflictions, undercurrents
of the messianic tradition continue in the occasional emergence of
revitalizing prophets inveighing against decadence and decay. At
this end of the spectrum I am sketching we clearly have the religion
of the Old Testament as well as those of the Nuer (Evans-Pritchard
1956) and the Dinka (Lienhardt 1961), where in the convenient
paradox of the one and the many, the spirits unequivocally represent man's experience of order and disorder in his universe.

This typological series traces the increasing involvement of prophets
in their surrounding social order until their revolutionary fervor is
almost completely dissipated. This suggests that the type of religion
that celebrates an accepted code of public morality can as readily
develop from as precede a messianic tradition. For it seems that in
the history of religions it is often possible to trace trends and developments in either direction through the various phases and points
of emphasis in our simple schema of spirit-possession and inspiration. And it is also perhaps necessary to stress, obvious though it is,
that to varying degrees several of the phases we have distinguished
may in fact coexist within a particular religious system at any given

time. Thus, to take a very simple example, although the principal emphasis in Somalia is on the engagement of possession in the "sex-war" in the manner I have described, there is also in that case a less significant but nonetheless coexistent organization of spirit medium coteries.

VII

Without attempting any very strict application of this model to the data discussed here, it may be worthwhile to indicate something more of the wider temporal and circumstantial setting of some of the cults with which we have dealt. Thus as Cerulli argues (1923: 2) the *zar* cult in Ethiopia today may well represent the ancient Cushitic religion centering on a sky-god displaced by Christianity and Islam and relegated to the status of a peripheral cult. In Somalia, however, there is no direct linguistic evidence for this assumption, and the cult there seems more securely regarded as an intrusive element. This certainly is the case with the affliction attributed to clerical sprites, which has only made its appearance within the last generation or so. In Arabia, the northern Sudan, and Egypt, the *zar* cult is likewise intrusive and of scarcely more than a century's standing (cf. Chapter 6). In its own local setting, the *bori* cult is generally regarded as the displaced traditional religion of the pre-Islamic Hausa, and there seems no good reason to dispute this view. In Haiti a rather similar relationship appears to have existed over several centuries between the slave and the later peasant cult of voodoo and of Christianity (Metraux 1959).

It seems probable that such displaced and peripherally relegated cults may provide the kind of institutional and inspirational continuity which, in appropriate historical circumstances, enables new messianic cults to develop and eventually to entrench themselves at the center of religious morality. This surely is one of the principal themes in the history of Christianity; and if the prophets of the Old Testament unquestionably herald Christ's messianic mission, the ultimate entrenchment of this religion in public morality in our own society, and the implicit disregard of eschatology except as a convenient metaphor for sanctioning good conduct, bring the cycle full circle. For the main public cult of nineteenth- and twentieth-century Christianity seems more in the morality-upholding spirit of the Old Testament than in the call-to-salvation spirit of the New Testament. Here we should also note the explicit refutation of the Church's traditional eschatology in the doctrines advanced by modern Christian apologists, who argue that heaven and hell are not realities in the traditional sense but rather existential states of mind.

By way of concluding, I would only add that we should also look more specifically at our own tradition of peripheral spirit-possession. In our religious history, the establishment of the Holy Spirit as the sole orthodox source of divine inspiration automatically disenfranchised other spiritual claims that could not be acceptably authenticated and exposed them to charges of fraud and traffic with the Devil, with consequences that we all know. This is the official view, exposed with characteristic casuistry in the late fifteenth-century *Malleus Maleficarum,* written by the Dominican authorities Kramer and Sprenger, which for at least two centuries seems to have served as the principal ecclesiastical guide on such matters. Although the increasingly liberal treatment by the Church of possession that was assigned to the work of Satan, and the rise of secularism and modern science in the nineteenth century, naturally fostered a widening of skepticism regarding peripheral spirit-possession, the phenomenon did not entirely disappear. Indeed, in the Victorian era, and especially after the challenge to orthodox theology presented by the publication in 1859 of Darwin's *Origin of Species,* a new upsurge of spiritualism claiming and to some extent receiving scientific approval made its appearance. This was the heyday of the Fox sisters and of the celebrated English medium Florence Cook, when as Trevor Hall aptly puts it, "as many heads as tables were being turned and the various interpretations put upon the mysterious dances of the furniture reflected the state of mind of those who advanced them. Spiritualists were certain that the tables moved under the influence of spirits; the clergy thought that this was probably true, but whether these discarnate entities were good or bad, angelic or demonic, was open to question" (Hall 1962: xi).

Although as the sustained current of spiritualist seances and publications indicates, spirit-possession in its traditional guise is, like other marginal mystical practices, by no means defunct today,[18] it can hardly claim the widespread interest and following it attracted among our grandparents. This decline seems to coincide fairly closely with the rise of modern psychology and psychoanalysis. And no one, I fancy, will question that many of the medical symptoms associated with spiritualism in our own past and in traditional societies are now treated on the psychoanalyst's couch. But perhaps this analogy can be pressed further. For at least in psychoanalysis, not only is the mode of entry to the profession broadly similar to that of the shaman's spiritual travail and apprenticeship, but the treatment situation of the patient is implicitly, and increasingly explicitly, psychodynamic in its essential characteristics. Certainly in the functional approach to psychiatric medicine so widely adopted today we have an interpretation of psychosomatic disorders – and according to some practitioners, of more serious mental maladies – that relates the patient's symptoms to his or her personal predicament by the same kind of contextual logic I have followed here.

In suggesting this comparison, I am not of course arguing that all psychological illness can properly be regarded as a response to deprivation, nor am I proposing that the whole of modern psychotherapy be viewed as a deprivation cult. The parallel seems best restricted to the incidence and treatment of the neurotic disorders, and particularly to psychosomatic and hysterical afflictions. Whatever other types of malady may be associated with tribal spirit-possession cults, these stand out as the most widely reported symptoms associated with peripheral possession. If the analogy I am proposing has some substance, it is therefore in this field of mental disorders that we should seek correlations between these afflictions and deprivation. Unfortunately, but not surprisingly in view of the difficulties involved in maintaining common standards of diagnosis, detailed statistical information on the epidemiology of mental illness in Western societies is not readily available. Nevertheless, a number of studies contain suggestive data. In their examination of mental illness in New Haven, Connecticut, Hollingshead and Redlich (1958) found a statistically significant *inverse* relationship between psychosomatic disorders and hysterical reactions on the one hand, and social class on the other. Disorders in these categories are most prevalent among the most socially deprived sections of the community. More recently, an analysis of diagnoses in neurosis cases from a sample of general practices in England showed an overwhelming predominance of female disorders: The reported ratio of female to male neurotic patients was two to one.[19]

In the present state of confusion in what it has now become fashionable to call transcultural psychology, it would be extremely naive to place too great reliance on such figures or to accept the parallel I have drawn without reservations. All I am suggesting, therefore, is that here is something worth considering further. In thus looking to psychology and psychiatry, as I think anthropologists must increasingly do (at least if we want to know the analogues in our own society of the syndromes that we examine and analyze in other cultures), I realize that I may offend those British colleagues who, whatever their declared theoretical affiliation, remain in practice faithful to the functionalism of Radcliffe-Brown, who was notoriously ambivalent toward psychology (see Lewis 1977). But lest I be too hastily condemned, let me be more explicit. In the psychologist's explanation of bizarre behavior in terms of unconscious motivation, projection, conversion, and the rest, I do not hope to find a final explanation of socially institutionalized behavior that closes the door to anthropological analysis. On the contrary, all I wish to do is to be able to classify and hold constant a range of similar symptoms which are dealt with in a wide diversity of institutionalized ways in different societies. I do not believe that *social* phenomena such as spirit-possession can be explained in terms of psychiatric illness or the malfunctioning of individual psyches. Nor, as I hope is clear, do I consider that a satisfactory explanation can be found in terms of dietary deficiencies (see Lewis 1983). My approach to the topic (which is no more "psychological" than that customarily adopted in the anthropological analysis of witchcraft and sorcery) assumes that all significant social behavior has an affective (i.e., "psychological") dimension. It is not possible to seek to understand spirit-possession in particular, any more than religion is general, without recognizing and acknowledging this.

3

Witchcraft within and without

I

The preceding chapter found it illuminating to examine spirit-possession from the viewpoint of the sociology of witchcraft. This chapter returns the compliment, suggesting that fresh light is shed on witchcraft when it is considered from the perspective we have developed for possession. In fact, as I trust will become plain, the process is mutually enlightening.

This can be seen at once when we turn to that recalcitrant problem in witchcraft studies — the fact that individuals sometimes spontaneously confess to being witches. In west Africa, particularly, it has long been noted that people sometimes voluntarily confess that they are witches and have bewitched others. This phenomenon where accuser and accused are the same person has become known as "introspective witchcraft" (see Field 1960; Ruel 1970) and has proved difficult to analyze within the framework of the standard structural-functionalist "anthropological" social tension theory of witchcraft (which of course is really psychological — see Lewis 1977). This theory assumes that the victim of misfortune seeks relief by accusing an enemy (the "witch") of responsibility for his or her ills. Introspective self-accusations, where accuser and accused are the same person, clearly do not fit easily into this scheme, and thus they constitute a problem.

Drawing on the approach to peripheral spirit-possession introduced in Chapter 2, however, R. W. Wyllie (1973) has developed a convincing analysis of introspective witchcraft in west Africa that is probably applicable elsewhere. In the southern Ghanian material he discusses, the witch is considered to act involuntarily, impelled against his or her will by the "fire within" (witchcraft) to endanger others. According to Wyllie, "Most of those who engage in self-accusation and confess to witchcraft are women and it is generally believed (and this is supported by their confessions) that their witchcraft, like that of child-witches, is always destructive and anti-social. Their confessions typically involve assertions that they have caused the death or illness of children (usually their own, but sometimes those of their brothers or sisters) by spiritually devouring the life-force or soul (*nkra*) of the victim" (Wyllie 1973: 76). A typical scenario involves an anxious mother obsessed by the witchcraft-urge to harm or kill her own baby.

Treatment (by traditional priests, witch-finders, or prophets) is a prolonged process. Confessions are heard during visits to a shrine at which the patient may be "hospitalized" for a time. Throughout the period of treatment for this particular cultural expression of what is known popularly in England as the "baby-bashing syndrome," the witch is visited regularly by relatives and friends bearing special items of food prescribed by the therapist. The cost of the treatment typically falls most directly on the husband of the witch. The cure, as Wyllie describes it, "involves personal recognition, consideration and attention from her husband and relatives who, through their supportive actions, demonstrate their appreciation of her worth and their desire that she should return to her place as a valued member of the household." Although by voicing destructive impulses toward her children the self-accused woman casts herself in the stereotyped role of "wicked mother," the involuntary character of her misdeeds provides her with immunity from blame. The parallels with our discussion of peripheral spirit-possession are striking and hardly require further elaboration.

It would of course be imprudent to suggest that all cases of witchcraft self-accusation conform to this pattern. But if the full significance and epidemiology of introspective witchcraft will require further research, it is nevertheless evident that this phenomenon constitutes a sort of halfway house between spirit possession and witchcraft that confirms the validity of a common sociological approach to both types of mystical aggression. From this perspective, we see peripheral spirit possession, "introspective" witchcraft and (shall we say) "extrovert" witchcraft and sorcery as responses to affliction that at the same time highlight problems in relationships. Because these varied forms of mystical aggression all explain affliction in terms of strained or broken relationships, we might be well advised, before proceeding further, to consider whether these responses to misfortune are mutually exclusive within a particular culture or society.

Those who approach this question from the direction of cosmology tend to answer it affirmatively. In his reflections on shamanism in the Nuba hills in the Sudan, for example, Nadel (1946: 34) concludes: "The Nyima have no witchcraft. Shamanism absorbs all that is unpredictable and morally indeterminate and saves the conception of an ordered universe from self-contradiction." Other anthropologists maintain similarly that if people believe that spirits can injure them out of pure malevolence, they hardly have need of the concept of an evil witch to fill out their view of the universe (see Mair 1969: 30).

This is an excessively narrow application of functionalist assumptions to cosmology and world view, one very typical of the curious but all too pervasive anthropological assumption that cultures and social systems are so economically and rigidly fashioned as to rule out alternatives, duplication, or repetition. The facts here, in any case, are quite the contrary. In many cultures, both witchcraft and malevolent spirit-possession of the kind discussed here do occur. This is true, for instance, among the Venda, and equally among the Kamba, BaThonga, Lenje, Zulu, Pondo, Valley Tonga, Luo, Lugbara, Banyoro, and Taita – to cite merely a few scattered African examples for which data are readily available. Indeed, the very common association of witchcraft with spirit-familiars – often of the opposite sex to the person possessed – is an obvious indication of the impossibility of regarding these mystical forces as mutually exclusive in any given society or culture. Nor is it necessary to look far afield for striking examples of the coexistence of witchcraft and spirit-possession. Our own sixteenth- and seventeenth-century Christian culture is abundantly rich in examples of witches whose malign power was intimately connected with invasive incubi and succubi.

It is thus evident that in many cultures these two forces coexist and sometimes blend into a hybrid phenomenon, as they do in effect with "introspective" witchcraft. That they should not be mutually exclusive at the level of individual cultures does not, of course, rule out the possibility that they might nevertheless have different impli-

Table 1. *Social contexts of peripheral possession and witchcraft*

People	Context of primary peripheral spirit-affliction is domestic domain, women vs. men	Context of witchcraft (sorcery) is generalized enmity, including that between co-wives
Akamba, BaThonga, Lenje, Taita, BaVenda, Zulu, Valley Tonga, Luo, Banyoro	Yes	Yes
Lugbara	?	Yes
Gurage	Yes*	?

* and subordinate Fuga versus freeborn Gurage men

cations or occur in contrasting social situations *within* a particular community. This suggests the hypothesis that if peripheral spirit possession and introspective witchcraft are found in similar social contexts and produce similar effects, "extravert" witchcraft (the bewitched victim accusing someone else of witchcraft) might be expected to occur in contrasting social contexts. This seems all the more likely in view of the distinction between possession and intro-spective witchcraft as *indirect* strategies of attack, on the one hand, and extravert witchcraft accusations as direct aggression on the other.

Table 1, which summarizes conveniently accessible evidence from a number of African cases, appears to confirm that indeed posses-sion and interpersonal witchcraft accusation typically occur in con-trasting social contexts. In the examples in the table, involuntary seizure by capricious peripheral spirits seems to be primarily restricted to the domestic domain, where it is employed by female dependents against their menfolk; sometimes, as with the Gurage in Ethiopia, it is also applied by male subordinates to bring pressure to bear upon superiors. Witchcraft and sorcery accusations, by contrast, appear to operate in a wider sphere of interaction and to occur in general contexts of animosity and hostility, particularly between equals, or between superior and subordinate. In those cases where witchcraft accusations are levelled by an inferior against a superior (as with the unpopular Lugbara elder), the intention seems to be to question the existing distribution of authority and ultimately to discredit the superior, casting him down from his pedestal and asserting equality. More specifically, in the polygynous family nexus, rivalry between co-wives characteristically takes the form of accusations of witchcraft or sorcery; in conflicts between husband and wife, the latter tends to resort to spirit-possession (or introspective witchcraft), the former to accuse his wife of witchcraft.

I do not claim that these distinctions are absolute, but I think that the evidence indicates trends in these two directions. This suggests that the oblique spirit-possession/introspective witchcraft strategy attempts to redress a painful situation by making claims for attention and demonstrations of regard from a superior without completely challenging the unequal relationship. It expresses insubordination, but not to the point where it is desired to sever the relationship or subvert it entirely. It ventilates aggression and frustration within the status quo. Witchcraft and sorcery accusations, by contrast, representing as they do a much more direct line of attack, express hostility between equal rivals, or between superior and subordinate (here reflecting the operation of spirit-possession in the reverse direction), and often seek to sunder an unbearably tense relationship (see Marwick 1965: 171–91). Thus, where they occur together in the same culture as alternative strategies, peripheral spirit-possession (or introspective witchcraft) usually offers a milder, less revolutionary line of attack, a less disruptive conflict strategy.

Consistent with these distinctions, possession-afflictions in wives do not normally seem to provide immediate grounds for divorce by the husband, whereas accusations of witchcraft directed against a wife may be used for this purpose. Thus, for example, among the South African Venda, where in the 1930s divorce was rare and not readily obtained, one of the special circumstances in which a wife could be divorced was when she had been designated a witch (Stayt 1931: 152). Again among the Venda, some indication of the relative strength and severity of the two lines of attack is provided by the fact that if peripheral spirit-possession actually led to a possessed woman's death, her husband could accuse his wife's mother of being a witch and demand and receive compensation for the killing (Stayt 1931: 305).

Finally, at the cosmological level also I think we can detect the same regular contrasts between the two types of power. Witchcraft and sorcery are regularly identified with incest, subversion, or even inversion of all commonly accepted moral values. In the popular folk view they represent the negation of morality and of normal social relations. The peripheral spirits with which we are concerned here, however, although also evil, are often not painted quite so black. Above all, they are capricious and mischievous, striking without any cause that can be directly referred to social relations or moral assumptions. In fact they seem to epitomize amorality rather than immorality: They stand completely outside society, inhabiting a world apart from that of men yet in many ways modeled on that of men. They typically range free in nature and are not subject to human constraints: They roam wild in the bush, are disaffiliated, inhuman, come from outside the culture in which they figure as sources of tribulation. All this seems consistent with the other distinctions we have noted between two modes of mystical attack.

II

So far I have been arguing that where spirit-possession and witchcraft are both found in the same culture they tend to be evoked in different social contexts and to have different social effects, although I admit that the differences may be only of degree. However, in many societies the situation is in reality more complex than this, since the two phenomena frequently merge or coalesce into a hybrid force, at least in some contexts.

Thus for example among the Lugbara in Uganda (Middleton 1969) there are two separate classes of diviners. The first, who are exclusively men and whom Middleton calls oracles, divine sickness caused by the ancestors in punishment of sins. The second, exclusively women or homosexual males, divine in cases of sickness ascribed to witchcraft or sorcery. These latter diviners, unlike their heterosexual male counterparts, are inspired through possession by peripheral spirits. From Middleton's earlier published data it is not clear to me whether spirit-possession also operates in the conjugal context discussed earlier, but it is surely highly significant that here we find spirit-possessed women enlisted as diviners in cases of witchcraft and sorcery that often arise in situations of lineage fission and lead to the erosion of the authority of established leaders (Middleton 1960). Among the Lugbara, such spiritually inspired divination is reported to be a recent innovation. This suggests that it may be interpreted as a kind of spiritual feminist movement having the effect of opening up new and highly significant avenues of social advancement for women.[1]

Whether or not this is a valid interpretation, here we see spirits enlisted in the fight against witches; whether diviners are also sometimes suspected of being themselves witches or sorcerers is not yet clear. However, in a number of other cases this association is definitely present. In Bunyoro, for instance, where it is evident from some of Beattie's case material (1961: 24) that peripheral spirit-possession may act as a restitutive mechanism in the conjugal situation, the same type of possession is also involved in one kind of sorcery and in divination (Beattie 1963: 44–5). Here "professional sorcerers" who sell their services to the public may also be spirit-inspired diviners, and sorcery can be employed either through the use of malevolently powerful *mahembe* horns or through medicines and techniques supplied by mediums possessed by peripheral spirits of foreign origin.[2] These latter "black" spirits seem to be increasing at the expense of the "white" *mbandwa* – the Cwezi "hero-gods" of the former legendary rulers of Bunyoro.

Again, among the Luo of Kenya, where a well-defined peripheral spirit-possession cult connected with women has been clearly described by Michael Whisson (1964), diviners may also be inspired by such spirits both to cure and to cause disease. In this case married women regularly succumb to possession-afflictions, bringing pressure on their husbands and in due course graduating to become spirit-possessed diviners. Those who thus come to control these spirits, however, may also use them in witchcraft against others. Much the same appears to be true in the case of the Lenje described by Earthy (1933: 196 ff.), where wives are armed by spirit-possession against their husbands and may also graduate in time to become mistresses of spirits operating both as diviners and as sorcerers (or witches). Male diviners, in contrast, practice in the context of the ancestor cult.

In dealing with this and other similar material it seems useful to distinguish between what might be called a "primary" and a "secondary" phase in the onset and socialization of possession. In the primary stage, women use "involuntary" and uncontrolled possession in the domestic domain as a recurrent means of coping with the stresses and difficulties of matrimony, for which they hold their husbands responsible. These difficulties are alleviated by gifts and special gestures of conciliation and consideration from the husbands. In the secondary phase, such women have graduated through membership in a regular possession coterie or cult group to become controllers of spirits. They now serve as therapists and diviners, thus assuming an active role that readily leads them to be accused of being witches or sorcerers. The factors that lead them into the second phase may relate to a radical change in the domestic situation (such as divorce or bereavement), or to some stage in the developmental cycle of the family. In any event, I suggest that the hostile reactions that primary-phase possession undoubtedly evokes on the part of men come to focus mainly on the secondary phase, in which possessed women, controlling their spirits, assume authoritarian roles that more directly threaten or challenge male authority. Hence the assumption that such diviners may be sorcerers (or witches); hence also the equation, controlled spirit-possession equals divination-sorcery (or witchcraft).

We should immediately add that this transformation of peripheral possession into witchcraft is not limited to repetitive phases within the developmental cycle of families. It may also correspond to socioeconomic changes affecting the relative status of men and women in a developing, and in essence irreversible, historical process. As Susan Reynolds Whyte (1981) points out, what is ultimately taking place here is a dialogue involving male and female discourses about power. This is dramatically reflected in the changing significance of the *avambakali* spirit cult of the Bashu in Zaire (Packard 1980). In the course of radical economic and political changes that have in some ways liberated women at the expense of men, these cannibalistic bush spirits have come to empower female witchcraft directed against men. In this form of mystical attack, *men* are possessed by these witchcraft familiars, which in the course of diagnosis and treatment directly implicate particular aggrieved women. The sanction of witchcraft accusation, however, is in this context by no means an unambiguously effective means of reasserting male dominance.

III

So far we have been concerned with possession by peripheral spirits as a response to tension experienced in different social contexts and its institutionalization in curing and divination by women who are liable to be concurrently suspected of being witches. In other cultures a further pattern of association between witchcraft and possession is evident.

Among the Pondo of South Africa, for example, witchcraft is quite unambiguously connected with possession by evil peripheral spirits. Witches are generally women and are inspired by obscene familiars – the *tokoloshe,* with their grotesquely large penises, through whose malign power they can illegitimately destroy life and property (Hunter 1936: 275–320). The concept of witchcraft here is very close to that prevalent in Europe between the fifteenth and seventeenth centuries – witches inspired by possessing incubi. As in European witchcraft, the possession of such familiars is taken as proof of witchcraft. Among the Pondo, however, it seems that no distinction is made between "primary" possession in the conjugal sphere and witchcraft at large; that is, there is no specialized female possession that can be distinguished from witchcraft and used against husbands in the marital context. Yet women also figure significantly as diviners, fighting witchcraft. In this case, however, they are possessed not by peripheral spirits (= witchcraft), but by the ancestors. Thus an unambiguous conceptual distinction is made between those spirits that animate witchcraft and those that inspire anti-witchcraft diviners, although both roles are generally taken by women. Antisocial malevolence is ascribed to the invasive peripheral spirits that possess witches; diviners owe their power to the ancestors who uphold customary morality. These female diviners thus act as auxiliary functionaries in the Pondo main morality cult of ancestors.

This clear-cut polarity between the sources of witchcraft and afflictions ascribed to its influence on the one hand and of ancestor-inspired diviners on the other is fairly closely paralleled among the Gusii (LeVine 1963). Much the same applies generally in Christian Ethiopia (Levine 1965:. 68ff.) and in those Philippine communities described by Lieban (1967) where sorcerers are inspired by malign peripheral spirits and diviners and healers by good spirits that are part of the main morality cult. In this case the cult is that of Latin Christianity and has not only morphological resemblances but also direct historical links with the older European tradition. Here I would only reiterate that, in its developed form, European witchcraft involved possession by devils, while power to treat the bewitched and to cast forth their satanic spirits lay with clerical exorcists inspired by Christ and the Holy Ghost. In practice, this ideologically rigid polarity was sometimes transcended in those not uncommon cases where exorcising priests themselves fell prey to the devils they sought to exorcise.

Hence there seem to be at least two patterns of connection between witchcraft (or sorcery) and spirit-possession. In the first, possession by peripheral spirits is the cause both of witchcraft and of anti-witchcraft divination and therapy, of affliction and its remedy. In the second, peripheral spirits animate only witchcraft; divination is inspired by powers that directly uphold social morality. The material discussed here suggests that, where peripheral possession has an unsolicited, *uncontrolled,* primary phase (as in the domestic situation), its *controlled* use in divination automatically associates the latter with witchcraft. Since it can be applied for good (divination) as well as for evil purposes (sorcery), there is no need to enlist the main morality powers as alternative sources of divinatory and curative inspiration. Where, however, the possessed person is not regarded as the helpless victim of the spirits but is believed to have solicited their support, and only a *controlled* nexus between possession and peripheral spirits is posited, it becomes necessary to enlist the main morality powers in divination and healing. In the first case, peripheral possession-afflictions are ultimately dealt with by taming and domesticating the spirit, by bringing it under control. When this happens, those who can control spirits and treat the afflicted are automatically suspected of being witches. In the second case, evil peripheral spirit-possession is treated by the exorcism of the afflicting spirit – by casting it out, not by taming it – and this requires the enlistment of superior mystical forces.

Indeed, in order to understand the action taken by the victim of affliction in securing an advantageous outlet for his distress – either through the medium of spirit-possession, "introspective witchcraft," or by accusing someone else of bewitching him – it may sometimes be more illuminating to discard the culturally grounded expressions "spirit-possession" and "witchcraft" altogether and to think instead in terms of oblique and direct mystical attack.

It may seem strange to speak of the action of the accuser, rather than that of the accused, as "mystical attack." But it is after all the accuser, not the accused witch, who sets the process in motion; and it is certainly the "witch" (the "extravert witch") against whom public opinion is mobilized and who is ultimately the victim of social action.

IV

If we adopt this broader analytic framework (which takes a further step along the comparative path, away from Evans-Pritchard's particularistic distinction between "witchcraft" and "sorcery"), it is obvious that witchcraft and witchcraft accusation is not the only mode of direct attack. Cursing also belongs here, and may be morally justified. Thus the contradictory facets of the Lugbara elder's role as legitimate invoker of the ancestor's curse and as suspected witch fall into place, and it becomes easier to understand those other cases of legitimately used "witchcraft" that anthropologists so often ignore or misconstrue (see Harwood 1970). Classic African examples of this situational – positive or negative – definition of what we colloquially call charisma include the Tiv concept *tsav*, a growth attached to the heart (Bohannon 1957); the Nyakyusa "python power" located in the stomach (Wilson 1951); and the Safwa concept *itonga*, excellently analyzed by Harwood (1970). All these represent mystical powers that the established authorities mobilize positively in the "national interest." But, when those in authority no longer command community support and lose control, these forces are redefined as their malign counterpart – antisocial, egotistical witchcraft.

In larger, centralized states, Wyatt MacGaffey (1970, 1972, 1980) has similarly pointed to the recurrent oscillation in African royal power between the morally approved, and therefore positive, use of mystical force in the "public interest" and its illegitimate abuse for antisocial "private interests" (= witchcraft). As in the earlier discussion of the complex linkage between spirit-possession and witchcraft (introvert and extravert), it is important to stress here the contextual moral relativity and fluidity of these positive and negative powers, especially if they seem completely unrelated phenomenologically. Thus in the Christian syncretist religion of Haitian voodoo, magically charged *points,* linked to deadly zombies, empower ambitious individuals to secure success at the expense of others. These antisocial forces are opposed by the benign family spirits – the "invisibles" (*loas*) which come from Africa, source of all good things. However, when a man dies, his personal store of magic *points* (associated with his achievements or charisma) becomes an ascribed part of the legacy he leaves to his heirs. They thus pass into the family patrimony and, becoming a collective (rather than individual) asset, are automatically transformed into *positive* power as benevolent "invisibles" (Larose 1977). As the context shifts diachronically from individual to communal interest, *cultural* magical artifacts thus become *natural* religion.

Thus we see that one form of "witchcraft" (where "witch" is self-accusing) is linked, in terms of its social implications as an oblique form of mystical attack, with peripheral spirit-possession. But spirit-possession is also linked through the role of the assertive diviner with witchcraft in its classic "extrovert" form (where accused and accuser are not the same person). The positive face of the latter is, in turn, legitimate mystical power. Positive charisma, we may say, is the acceptable face of witchcraft, and witchcraft the unacceptable face of charisma[3] — that corrupt power so trenchantly delineated in Lord Acton's famous aphorism.

4

The cannibal's cauldron

I

As William Arens (1979) has persuasively argued, anthropologists are often remarkably casual and uncritical in their treatment of reports of cannibalism in exotic cultures. Disregarding the usual methodological prerequisite of firsthand observation – enshrined in the Malinowskian fieldwork manifesto – our accounts of cannibalism all too frequently rely on secondhand reports. Such lack of scholarly rigor regularly leads to the confusion and conflation of the idea or ideology of cannibalism with its actual practice. Hence, many modern anthropological studies inadvertently tend to entrench and further legitimize deep-seated Eurocentric assumptions concerning the prevalence of cannibalism in tribal societies. Although few of the anthropologists involved here would see it in this light, they thus implicitly maintain the tradition of Freud, who in his magnificent cosmic fable *Totem and Taboo* ([1913]; 1950) casually introduced cannibalism to embellish his theory of primordial incest. In the Freudian version of the Oedipus myth, once liberated by the murder of their tyrannical father the rebellious sons, being "cannibal savages," celebrated the event by *eating* him. The subsequent regularly performed ritual slaughter and eating of the totemic animal, which replaced the murdered father, commemorated and replicated the original act of parricidal cannibalism. According to Freud (1950: 142) these hypothetical events marked the crucial turning point in man's evolutionary development – the "beginning . . . of social organization, of moral restrictions and of religion."

In fact, the application of the derogatory label "man-eater" is one of the most widely distributed methods by which the members of one group or community dissociate and distance themselves from outsiders beyond the pale. Cannibalism, however, *pace* Arens (1979: 145ff.), is much more than merely a matter of labeling and stigmatizing disparaged groups and individuals. The ideology of man-eating provides a pregnant cluster of imagery and metaphor to express the exercise and experience of power, domination, and subjection which may be realized in different forms in particular historical and cultural contexts. The appellation "cannibal" is not merely an appropriate term of contempt for uncouth subjects at the bottom of the political hierarchy or on the edge of the civilized world. It may be applied equally appropriately by the victims of oppression to designate their superiors. The designation "cannibal" can thus convey a sense of impotence and desperation and is consequently not always flattering to its user. Again, the term may be employed reciprocally between antagonistic parties of equal status and rank. In this chapter we explore this inherently double-edged imagery, arguing that both in theory and in practice cannibalism ultimately derives its perennial fascination and pervasive evocative power from intimate physical experiences common to all human beings. Although psychoanalytic insights may be helpful here, it is thus unnecessary, *pace* Epstein (1979), to invoke particular childhood traumas or culturally specific child-rearing practices in order to understand the phenomenon.

II

The orthodox anthropological approach to the social dynamics of witchcraft, which we sought to expand in the previous chapter, assumes a disinterested (if not disbelieving) external perspective that concentrates upon the accusation and the *accuser* rather than upon the *accused* witch. In the case of cannibalism, an inadvertent personal experience of the author's – shared with Arens and others – reverses the equation and so provides serendipitous food for thought. Traveling in the remote Ndembu countryside of western Zambia (then Northern Rhodesia) in the late 1950s, I personally experienced and still vividly recall the suspicion and fear with which lonely African pedestrians responded to offers of lifts in my Land Rover. Their stock reaction was to disappear swiftly into the nearby bush. The explanation for this rather striking avoidance behavior, I discovered, was the assumption, widely prevalent in central Africa at that time, that many Europeans were vampire-men who sucked the blood and ate the flesh of innocent Africans. Similar concepts about cannibalistic Europeans flourished with varying degrees of intensity in east Africa (see Friedland 1960), southern Africa, and in the Congo, where during the Belgian period in Leopoldville the white vampire was known as the "man with the lamp." Around the same time (1958) an unsuspecting European firm in the Belgian Congo marketed canned meat in cans with labels depicting chubby, smiling African babies. The product was not an unqualified success.

A similarly mixed reception greeted the appearance in Northern Rhodesia during this period of cans of cheap meat designed for the local African work force market and labeled "For African Consumption" (see Fraenkel 1959). The ill-fated British plan to form a multiracial Central African Federation joining Northern Rhodesia and Nyasaland (now Malawi) to white-settler dominated Southern Rhodesia (Zimbabwe) had aroused deep and widespread suspicion and alarm among the African population. Africans accustomed to the relatively benign paternalistic colonial administrations of Northern Rhodesia and Nyasaland feared that the proposed federation would involve an extension to their territories of the pattern of white supremacy characteristic at that time of Southern Rhodesia. Since the majority of the population were cultivators, there was particularly acute anxiety that traditional land rights would be endangered by an influx of European farming interests from Southern Rhodesia (Watson 1958; Epstein 1958, 1979). In such an atmosphere of mistrust, and with the failure of African political pressure to prevent the establishment in 1953 of the Federation (doomed to collapse six years later under the weight of African opposition), rumors quickly spread in Northern Rhodesia that the meat marked "For African Consumption" contained human flesh specially doctored to break down African resistance to the unpopular policy of federation. Seeking to counter such fears, a European district commissioner on the Northern Rhodesian copper belt publicly consumed the meat to prove that it was harmless. This demonstration almost certainly had the paradoxical effect of confirming rather than allaying general African fears that Europeans were cannibals. Nor was African public opinion on this issue likely to be disabused by the conviction, about this time, in a European court in Nyasaland, of an African accused of trying to sell two well-fattened children to a European for his Christmas dinner.[1]

In some parts of Africa, as in other European colonies, it appears possible to trace a link between this view of Europeans as cannibalistic blood-suckers and blood donation campaigns. Sometimes these ideas are (or were) associated through the color red, with European-introduced fire services and fire stations (while still novel) acquiring a sinister reputation as centers for extracting and collecting the African blood believed to be consumed by Europeans to sustain their vitality (Friedland 1960). Similarly, in Northern Rhodesia rural health campaigns involving blood tests have sometimes precipitated outbreaks of panic, during which consumption of tinned tomato juice by Europeans has been taken as further proof of their lust for blood. More recently, in southern Africa as a whole, it does not require much imagination to grasp the further medical confirmation of these ideas provided by reports of Dr. Christian Barnard's transplant surgery, utilizing in some cases hearts from African bodies to give new life to whites.

In the more distant past, there is direct evidence that African fears about the vampire propensities of Europeans are also in part a reflection of the slave trade. And it is ironic to note that both the Arabs and the Europeans involved in this traffic appear to have spread rumors accusing each other of practicing cannibalism.[2] Such allegations naturally helped to reinforce and extend the existing indigenous belief in the reality of cannibalism, associating it, in particular, with rapacious invaders.

III

These factors, however, do not alone suffice to explain how Africans came to suspect Europeans of being cannibals. To understand this fully we have to set cannibalism in context as part of a wider constellation of ideas concerning mystical power in general and witchcraft in particular. It is obviously significant that Europeans were believed by Africans not only to indulge in cannibalism but also to practice witchcraft. From an African perspective, it was largely *because* Europeans were seen as witches that they were liable to be suspected of practicing cannibalism. Witches, as we know, employ sinister forces to achieve selfish ends to the disadvantage of virtuous citizens and neighbors. Success – in the "limited good" witchcraft scenario (cf. Foster 1965) – is at the expense of others. The witch, consequently, inevitably becomes endowed with all the antisocial vices that are the counterparts of corresponding social virtues. Hence the inverted witch stereotype includes all manner of sexual perversion, incest, and the ultimate denial of human sociability and commensality – cannibalism. "Witches eat people," as the Nso of Cameroon (Kaberry 1969), the Shona of Zimbabwe (Crawford 1967), and many other peoples succinctly state. Indeed, the statement, "A witch is a cannibal," is one of the more widely current minimum definitions of the witch role.

Those who define the epitome of evil in this way also believe that the mystical forces that so enable ambitious, unscrupulous individuals to achieve more than their fair share of life's good things can, in other contexts, be used positively in the general interest. As we emphasized in the previous chapter, what anthropologists regularly translate from other cultures by the English term "witchcraft" (or the French *"sorcellerie"*) is, on closer inspection, typically ambiguous. Those whom English anthropologists describe as socially approved "witch doctors" because of their expertise in combating and countering illicit witchcraft usually owe their success to causing what they cure. Here the negative side empowers the positive side which legitimates it. The "python power" of the Nyakyusa (referred to earlier) both provides the basis of witchcraft and empowers the positive righteous indignation of the village elders to defend the local community against external threat. Similarly, as we saw, the mystical force that enables the elders among the Tiv of Nigeria to uphold morality and protect their community is equally the source of malevolent witchcraft. A Tiv witch seeks to obtain selfish aims at the expense of others, and to secure success nourishes his *tsav* on a diet of human flesh – cannibalism again becoming a critical element in the definition of "witch." In precisely the same vein, unpopular Amazonian shamans are denounced as "witches" practicing cannibalism against their own people – aggressive shamanic power in the Amazon generally being associated with the anaconda and jaguar (Lévi-Strauss 1966; Reichel-Dolmatoff 1971; Hugh-Jones 1980; Colajanni 1982; Seymour-Smith 1984).

So too accusations of abuse of power (implying, as we have seen, witchcraft) leveled today against African government ministers and chiefs may include the denunciation "cannibal" (cf. MacCormack 1983). Here we need again recall the equivocal nature of power and its mystical implications. What was typically involved was essentially control over the ruler's subjects and lands, whose fecundity was affected by the chief's mystical energies, which had always to be protected and maintained at the requisite level of effectiveness. In Africa, as elsewhere, leaders were expected to have sex appeal. There was always some connection, however concealed, between such political sexuality and the fertility of people and land. The Bemba of Zambia illustrate these themes with unusual directness. Their kings, members of the ruling clan (whose totem is the man-eating crocodile), were expected regularly to perform ritual sexual intercourse with their wives in order to promote the prosperity of their land and its inhabitants (Richards 1968).

It is against such traditional attitudes toward power (which, as Balandier remarks, is never completely emptied of religious content) that we should understand the conviction, widespread in colonial Africa, that Europeans were cannibalistic witches. The superior military and material technology of the white man, the sources of which were unfamiliar and often mysterious; his miraculous healing medicines; the Christian religion, which underpinned his moral superiority and helped him to maintain law and order in adverse conditions: all these inevitably suggested that the European possessed a unique store of mystical power. If some aspects of European colonial rule were perceived as beneficial, others were not; and, here as elsewhere, the exercise of authority always engendered some resentment against the rulers. What is involved here is more complex than simply colonial exploitation.

African suspicions concerning the sinister roots of European power received additional support from the way in which European colonial administrations and missions reacted to traditional African beliefs in witchcraft (and sorcery). Proclaiming that witches did not exist, European administrations had typically made it illegal for Africans to accuse or punish suspected witches. Legislation proscribing witchcraft accusations was introduced throughout British Africa. The Southern Rhodesia Witchcraft Suppression Act of 1899 is a typical example from the region that is our primary focus here. The act is primarily concerned to prevent "imputations" of witchcraft, as the following extracts indicate:

> In this Act "witchcraft" includes the "throwing of bones," the use of charms and other means or devices adopted in the practice of sorcery.

Whoever imputes to any other person the use of non-natural means in causing any disease in any person or animal or in causing any injury to any person or property, that is to say, whoever names or indicates any other person as being a wizard or witch shall be guilty of an offence and liable to a fine not exceeding two hundred dollars or to imprisonment for a period not exceeding three years, or to whipping not exceeding twenty lashes or to any two or more of such punishments.

Whoever, having so named and indicated any person as a wizard or witch, is proved at his trial under section three to be by habit and repute a witch doctor or witch finder shall be liable, on conviction, in lieu of the punishment provided by section three to a fine not exceeding five hundred dollars or to imprisonment for a period not exceeding seven years or to whipping not exceeding thirty-six lashes or to any two or more of such punishments.

As Gordon Chavunduka, the first black African professor of sociology at the University of Zimbabwe,[3] observes, the aim of this act is not to punish witches but those who expose witches (by making witchcraft accusations), and consequently in rural Zimbabwe it is regarded today as a "very unjust piece of legislation" (Chavunduka 1980: 130). In a similar fashion, in French Africa, the *Code Penal Indigene* and later the *Code Napoleon* outlawed witchcraft accusations (cf. Alexandre 1974). The effect, of course, of such colonial legislation and its implementation in administrative (and sometimes "native") courts was to *protect* witches and to suppress legitimate means of exposing witchcraft. For those believing in witchcraft the obvious conclusion to draw was that the European rulers were on the side of the witches – and hence, indeed, given all the other aspects of their political superiority, "super-witches." This seems to me the most potent factor in the train of circumstantial evidence leading to the ascription of cannibalistic witchcraft to Europeans (including unsuspecting anthropologists).[4]

IV

It is ironic that those who do not believe in witchcraft should as a result be suspected of practicing it. Cannibalism, on the other hand, is often not practiced by those believed by anthropologists to be cannibals. This strange anthropological paradox, which despite their close connection treats witchcraft and cannibalism so differently, reflects the outright disbelief with which reports of witchcraft are usually received, in contrast to the reception usually accorded reports of cannibalism. The stock anthropological response to the juxtaposition of the two is very revealing. Firmly believing that witchcraft does not exist, anthropologists are likely to dismiss as pure fantasy reports of acts of cannibalism in a witchcraft context. In other contexts, the response to reports of cannibalism is often much less critical.

This intriguing contrast in emphasis and interpretation (paralleling that already noted in Chapter 3 in the treatment of witchcraft and spirit-possession) can be seen in what still remains the most comprehensive and subtle anthropological analysis of witchcraft – Evans-Pritchard's magisterial work on the Azande of the southern Sudan and Congo, to which we have already referred (Chapter 2). If the reality of witchcraft is unacceptable to Evans-Pritchard, there is no question of the reality of accusations of witchcraft, since these can be readily observed and the associated diagnostic rituals and alleviating procedures recorded in minute detail. The famous Zande distinction (to which we have already referred) between "sorcery" as an objective physical technique and "witchcraft" as a psychic force, also happens to accord with Evans-Pritchard's Eurocentric, objective bias. This distinction, in turn, appears to have led Evans-Pritchard to emphasize the unintentional, unpremeditated aspects of Zande witchcraft as an unconscious phenomenon at the expense of the conscious, deliberate aspects that are uppermost in the mind of the bewitched accuser. Although he presents detailed evidence for both these contradictory facets, this at least is how the overall picture of Zande witchcraft has usually been "read";[5] and it is, I suggest, in harmony with the broader distinction between witchcraft and sorcery.

It is not unreasonable to suggest that Evans-Pritchard's own disbelief in witchcraft helps him to investigate with admirable detail and precision the complex issue of Zande skepticism – a topic almost completely ignored in the same author's celebrated account of the theistic beliefs of the Nuer (published after his conversion to the Catholic faith).[6] Confident as he was in discounting the efficacy claimed for witchcraft by the Zande, Evans-Pritchard was more cautious in his assessment of references to Zande cannibalism. Having subjected earlier travelers' allegations to devastating and caustic criticism, he nevertheless felt it imprudent to dismiss them entirely, on the grounds that "there is no smoke without fire" (Evans-Pritchard 1965: 153).

Here, as usual, much turns on the accurate rendering of native statements and so on translation, which, as is well-known, Evans-Pritchard himself saw as the crux of the anthropological endeavour. A more recent study of Zande mystical beliefs by the Austrian anthropologist Manfred Kremser (1981) sheds important new light on this problem. Kremser shows that the term *kawa,* translated into English as "human meat" and usually taken in the Zande literature as evidence of cannibalism, relates primarily to the witchcraft domain. Thus the witch may attack his victim by extracting the latter's life force (*kawa*), putting it in a pot, and typically hanging the pot with its contents on a tree. This is a state of raw suspense. For if this *kawa* is cooked and eaten, the bewitched victim can never recover. If, however, events do not proceed to this irreversible conclusion and the *kawa* remains uncooked and unconsumed, the witch can be persuaded to unbind this life essence from the branch and restore it to the bewitched victim, who is then expected to recover. Curiously, as far as I have been able to determine, Evans-Pritchard's richly documented study of Zande witchcraft does not contain any mention of *kawa* and does not explore this important relationship between the process of witchcraft attack (which he refers to as "vampirism") and cannibalism. This specific linkage, however, is clearly present in a text which in Evans-Pritchard's translation (1937: 35) includes the following passage: "Witches arise and beat their drum of witchcraft. The membrane of this drum is human skin. . . . Their drum call is 'human flesh, human flesh, human flesh.' " Although Evans-Pritchard does not tell us this, it would thus appear that *one* of the sources for the imputation of cannibalism to the Zande rests on the (metaphorical or psychic) consumption of "human flesh" extracted from their victims by witches.

V

More generally, this contrasting anthropological treatment of witchcraft and cannibalism, and the ironical readiness on the part of some anthropologists to view as cannibals those who are prone to view Europeans in the same light, cannot of course be explained in quite the same terms as our central African examples. We can understand the anthropological disbelief in witchcraft more easily than the anthropological belief in cannibalism. The functionalist William Arens (1979: 184), appropriately enough, has proposed a functionalist explanation for his colleagues' lingering credulity. The appellation *cannibal,* he argues, continues to have wide exotic appeal. As the study of cannibals, anthropology is thereby made to seem more exciting. At the same time, anthropologists have a professional interest in maintaining their uniquely privileged role as the specially licensed mediators between their Western world and the exotic alien cultures which, through the imputed stigma of cannibalism, help define the boundaries of Western civilization.

I do not dissent at all from this view of the exploitative, entrepreneurial role of anthropology and anthropologists (cf. Lewis 1976: 34). But to claim, as Arens does, that in general the concept "cannibal" primarily functions as a boundary marker or label distinguishing "us" (non-cannibals) from "them" (cannibals) hardly does justice to the relevant data. The suggestion (Arens 1979: 145) that groups of similar culture have *more* need to resort to the distancing (not-us) label "cannibal" is interesting, but not substantiated – and in fact appears unconvincing. Arens seems also to imagine that since witchcraft does not exist (except as a reality of thought) the same applies to the linked concept of cannibalism, which must therefore be accorded the same mythical status.[7] This perspective on cannibalism is clearly biased in the direction of the negative aspects of witchcraft and takes little or no account of mystical ambivalence or positive charisma. To reach a more balanced and comprehensive view, we must acknowledge that when people interpret the actions of others in terms of cannibalism, they are making statements of more pervasive significance than mere intellectual labeling. As Sahlins (1983: 88) cogently puts it: "Cannibalism is always 'symbolic' even when it is real." To proceed further, we should, I believe, pay close attention to body symbolism, recognizing the extent to which the biological functions of the human body provide a fertile matrix for potently charged ("natural") symbols.

In applying this perspective to cannibalism we should begin by noting that its most general cultural context – either as idea or as actual practice – is usually a ritual setting. Here, where a tabooed negative action – eating human flesh – acquires positive force, the ritual consumption of parts of the human body enables the consumer to acquire something of the body's vital energy. Ritual can-

nibalism (as indeed Arens himself recognizes) is consequently a form
of sacrificial communion. Indeed, it is perhaps *the* prototype of sacrificial communion, since as Sahlins[8] maintains (no doubt correctly)
"cannibalism exists *in nuce* in most sacrifice." As is well-known,
this has very powerful resonance in the Christian Eucharist, where
according to the official doctrine communicants consume the bread
and wine that through the miracle of transubstantiation becomes
the flesh and blood of Christ. The case of cannibal converts to
Christianity is thus particularly poignant, as Sahlins, referring to
nineteenth-century missionary accounts in the Marquesas, trenchantly observes.

The Trobriand Islanders practiced a more direct and lurid form
of commemorative cannibalism than the Eucharist (Malinowski
1929: 133). The body of a deceased man was exhumed and dis-
membered by his sons and other (nonmatrilineal) relatives. Although,
as Malinowski observed, the mourners found this extremely repugnant, they were expected to display their filial piety by sucking the
decaying flesh of the corpse they were dismembering. The bones
were conserved as relics commemorating the dead, reverently
wrapped in dry leaves, and finally deposited on rocky shelves over-
looking the sea. With subtle changes of symbolic emphasis, similar
practices are reported elsewhere in Melanesia. Until as recently as
1950, for example, the Gimi of the New Guinea highlands practiced what might be called compassionate cannibalism. Women were
expected to eat the dead bodies of their men in order to release the
latters' individual spirits, freeing them to rejoin the collective body
of ancestral forest spirits. According to Andrew Strathern (1982:
125), as they ate the men's bodies women used to sing seductively,
"Come to me lest your body rot in the ground. Better it should
dissolve inside me." There is a significant emphasis on sexual antag-
onism and sexuality here, to which we shall return shortly. For in
releasing the men's spirits by consuming their bodies, the women
are also considered to be exacting vengeance on men for stealing
the penislike initiation flutes that the women originally possessed.

This sexual complementarity is further elaborated in the complex
mortuary cannibalism of another New Guinea people, the Bimin-
Kuskusmin described by Fitzjohn Porter Poole (1983). Here, male
agnates honor the dead, counteracting the pollution of the mortuary rites by eating morsels of the (male-substance) bone marrow of

the deceased. This ensures the passage of the dead man's spirit to the ancestral underworld and the recycling of his procreative and ritual strength within his patrilineage. Female agnates eat small pieces of lower belly fat (female substance) to enhance their reproductive and ritual powers. Although it is considered particularly disgusting, penis flesh is even presented to the widow, the eating of which is believed to enhance her fertility and bind her productive power to the agnatic kin of the deceased husband. Reciprocally, the ritually active husband of a dead woman is expected to eat a fragment of her sexual organ so as to enhance the fertility of her daughters. In all these funeral contexts, the stress is on ensuring the fertility and continuity of a group weakened by death. On the battlefield, however, Bimin-Kuskusmin warriors add insult to injury, expressing their contempt for defeated foes by eating the feminine portions of their corpses and thus preventing them from achieving full ancestor status (Porter Poole 1983: 15).

This brings us to the classical political context of cannibalism in the agonistic relations between hostile groups, the prime sacrificial victims being war captives or slaves (often similarly recruited). In this vein, Maori cannibalism − well-documented from contemporary nineteenth-century eyewitness accounts − was set in a context of ritual warfare; the consumption of human flesh paralleled that of birds and fish in hunting rituals. Men consumed at cannibalistic feasts were referred to as "fishes," and "first fish" being eaten by a chief who thus acquired control over the land of the vanquished. Victorious Maori chiefs are reported to have increased their *mana* by swallowing the eyes of their enemies.[9] In Fiji during the same period, chiefs of reputedly immigrant origin received tribute in the form of what Sahlins (1983: 80) calls "raw" women and supplied "cooked" men in communion feasts as largesse in return. The resources for this system of noblesse oblige were typically war captives or "internal" aliens in the form of rebels and dissidents. These sacrificial victims, "food for the gods," assumed divine status and were accorded the same terms of ritual reference as the body of a chief.

The ideas and symbols in play here achieve their most elaborate realization in Amazonian Indian ritual cannibalism. The Tupi-namba of Brazil have long provided the locus classicus, known to Western scholars from the extensive, carefully documented sixteenth-century eyewitness accounts of the Portuguese Jesuit missionaries. Although Arens has attempted to discredit this picture of Tupi cannibalism by questioning the evidence in some of the more sensational popular accounts, the cumulative testimony is overwhelming and very convincing,[10] as Donald Forsyth (1983) has recently demonstrated in an impressively rendered reappraisal of the firsthand Jesuit evidence. The picture that emerges in these accounts is that the Tupi practiced ritual cannibalism extensively in the context of war and vengeance raids. Among the Tupinamba, who in common with so many other people married their enemies, a war captive was called a "loved one." Such prisoners, potential affines like the Tupi gods, were feted, provided with unmarried women as companions, and enjoyed luxury prisoner status for extended periods before they were ritually executed and consumed in an often orgiastic communion feast. Thus at the heart of the most sumptuous ritual cannibalism we encounter the theme of sexuality, which is also present in witchcraft. This is no coincidence. I do not think that we can reach any general understanding of the meaning and pervasive appeal of the ideology of cannibalism, and its use in labeling others and in interpreting their activities, unless we take due note of these sexual allusions.

As is well-known, eating and sexuality are closely related modes of intimate social interaction that readily flow together, both literally and metaphorically. In many, perhaps most, languages, including to some extent English, the same or similar expressions are used to refer to eating and making love. Consumed with desire, the lover eagerly seeks to devour the object of his passion. Terms of endearment, likewise, regularly compare the love object to a tempting dainty dish. In the contemporary Western world this equivalence or concurrence of the two modes of commensality – eating and sex – is appropriately reflected in the striking similarity in style and format between gourmet sex manuals and cookbooks. Some sex manuals, indeed, literally set out the stages of amorous play in the form of a menu; and sexual and culinary recipes lie side by side in the pages of journals like *Penthouse* and *Playboy.* Common expressions relating to love and sexual intercourse, such as "conquest" and "match," bear an obvious aggressive charge that is also present in the competitive elements of feasting and hospitality. In some African contexts, political usurpation is said to be represented as a process of seduction with the aid of tempting food.[11] In Fiji, according to Sahlins (1983: 79), a lowly commoner would grovel before a chief with the obeisance, "Eat me." Elsewhere "Be my guest!" is apt to be a challenge as well as an invitation. It is consequently scarcely necessary to refer to love bites, or *vagina dentata,* or indeed to the intermittent Western vogue for oral sex, to evoke the image of Dracula, the pan-human vampire, who so vividly embraces all these themes.

Ernest Jones[12] certainly recognized these parallels when he identified what he termed "oral sadism" in the concept of the vampire. For him this was a "regressive complex," provoked by the repression of normal adult genital sexuality. A typical if tragic illustration at the individual level would presumably be the case of the "cannibal of the Bois de Boulogne," the Japanese student in Paris who confessed to shooting and then eating an attractive Dutch girl who had rebuffed his advances and refused to sleep with him.[13] This is the sort of "abnormal" case that the psychoanalytic anthropologist Georges Devereux (1956) would no doubt characterize as "ego-dystonic." But a diagnosis of cannibalism, where it is a culturally accepted practice, as "culture dystonic" and hence indicative of general cultural malaise, is unlikely to appeal to the cultural-relativist anthropologist (cf. Geertz 1984). Similarly, Ernest Jones's rigid Freudian schema of evolutionary stages of sexual aggression seems today an excessive piece of psychoanalytic dogma. We surely no longer need to invoke the ideas of "regression" and "repression" to acknowledge a more flexible framework in which the different modes of sexuality interpenetrate and flow into each other. From this perspective, linked as they are to oral and genital sexual aggression, the ideas of consumption, ingestion (see Porter Poole 1983), engulfment, and mastery clearly constitute potent symbols of power. Rooted in the universal human experiences of suckling, engaging in sex, and eating, these motifs provide the most pervasive thematic and emotional matrix for everything that pertains to the general phenomenon of cannibalism. It is therefore hardly surprising that, even when the practice of cannibalism has disappeared or has never existed, the *idea* of man-eating should survive as a latent force always capable, so long as beliefs in mystical power are sustained, of being evoked in myth and popular fantasy. The problem is not, as Arens (1979: 139) claims, that of explaining why people attribute cannibalism to their neighbors and enemies, but rather of understanding those cultures in which cannibalism is (or was) actually practiced as an integral part of ritual life. Here, as usual in the analysis of cultural forms, we may discern general thematic patterns associated with symbolic meanings recurring in similar ritual contexts. To attribute these, or other aspects of institutionalized culture, to such simple materialist "causes" as protein deficiency (Marvin Harris 1977), is in my opinion patently absurd.

5

The shaman's career

I

The term *shaman* belongs to that special category of ethnographically specific concepts used cross-culturally outside their own native contexts. Other such "-emic" terms are, of course, *caste, compadrazgo, mana, potlatch, tabu,* and perhaps *totem* and *voodoo.* These constitute a small but interesting category of originally culturally specific terms whose use, outside their native context, regularly engenders controversy and debate.

Although as Vilmos Voigt (1977: 385) justly observes in his admirable bibliographical critique, the "word shaman and the word Shamanism spread all over the world from Siberia," the currency of these terms varies considerably among the different national (and international) anthropological traditions and partly reflects regional ethnographic specialization. They are well represented in the Scandinavian,[1] East European,[2] and continental traditions,[3] although perhaps less frequently in France.[4] In Italy, S. M. Shirokogoroff's classic account of Tungus shamanism, discussed later in this chapter, encouraged the influential historian of religion and man of letters Ernesto de Martino to launch a vigorous – and in his milieu at the time (1942) bold – attack on European ethnocentrism that ran contrary to the neo-Hegelian tradition of his own spiritual mentor, Benedetto Croce.[5]

In Anglophone anthropology, as so often elsewhere, there is a marked contrast here between American and British usage. With its Arctic (Eskimo) connections[6] and traditional Amerindian bias (more recently reinforced by South American studies), and with the blessing of such founding fathers as Franz Boas,[7] the term "shaman" enjoys a secure position in American cultural anthropology. This is not the case in Britain, where the dominant structural-functionalist school has emphasized the contrasting concept *spirit-possession,* leaving shamanism to be subsumed under (or discarded as superfluous in distinction to) *spirit mediumship.* So, for instance, Godfrey Lienhardt's sensitive account of religious enthusiasm among the Dinka of the southern Sudan, *Divinity and Experience* (1961), contains more than twenty indexed references to possession – but not one to shamans or shamanism. If this had been the work of an American anthropologist, I suspect the terminology would have been rather different. Under such different ethnic sponsorship, Dinka shamans would surely by now have achieved a secure place in the ethnographic record.

The well-known British anthropologist S. F. Nadel's (1946) application of the term "shamanism" to the religious beliefs and practices of the peoples of the Nuba Hills of the Sudan is thus the exception that proves the rule (although it could perhaps be argued that Nadel had a more "continental" intellectual background than most of his contemporary British colleagues). The orthodoxy was, and remains, quite clear. Among mainline British social anthropologists and those American and other anthropologists strongly influenced by them,[8] concern continues over the propriety of the term "shaman," and it is consequently treated with grave reserve and used with marked reluctance. Following such earlier ventures as J. Beattie and J. Middleton's *Spirit Mediumship and Society in Africa* (1969), two recent symposia,[9] published in English but including contributions by French as well as American authors, similarly eschew the term "shamanism" in their titles – although the topic does materialize in their texts.

This hesitancy to accept the terms "shaman" and "shamanism" into standard British anthropological currency seems consistent with our emphasis on comparative analysis, our focus on societies rather than cultures, and our preference for "-etic" rather than *"-emic"* categories. We like to think that by employing external analytical terms having no cultural undercurrent except in our own English tradition we achieve greater precision and clarity and so avoid cultural confusion. Actually, however, as is becoming increasingly clear, such analytical categories become charged with an implicit cultural loading of their own derived from the exotic ethnographies to which we apply them. Even when we do not directly apply local folk categories outside their cultural contexts, we find that ethnographic regions still leave their imprint on our analytical vocabulary and color our theorizing. The pervasive, if not always persuasive, influence of Evans-Pritchard's use of Zande views of witchcraft and sorcery, or of Nuer lineages, has already been cited in this regard (Chapter 1).

With the transient exception of Nadel, the one major British anthropologist who has employed the term "shaman" is Raymond Firth – mainly to indicate a distant point on the horizon. Thus Firth (1967: 296) scrupulosuly distinguishes between "spirit-possession," "spirit mediumship," and "shamanism." Spirit-possession, Firth says, involves "phenomena of abnormal behaviour which are interpreted by other members of society as evidence that a spirit is controlling the person's actions and probably inhabiting his body." In "spirit mediumship" the accent, as Firth puts it, is on communication. Finally "shamanism," Firth states, "applies to those phenomena where a person, either a spirit medium or not, is regarded as controlling spirits, exercising his mastery over them in socially recognised ways."

II

These distinctions seem at least to some extent to reflect the widespread influence of Mircea Eliade's magisterial work, *Le chamanisme et les techniques archaiques de l'extase* (1951). Eliade here purports to take us back to the Siberian Tungus ethnography, to which the word shaman is usually traced etymologically.[10] The shaman in this context is an inspired priest who in ecstatic trance states ascends, in spirit or soul, to the heavens on mystical "trips." He there meets and communes with the celestial powers in order to advance the interests of his fellow men. Spirit-possession is not directly connected with this. For Eliade "the specific element of shamanism is not the incorporation of spirits by the shamans but the ecstasy provoked by the ascension to the sky or by the descent to hell: the incorporation of spirits and possession by them are universally distributed phenomena, but they do not belong necessarily to shamanism in the strict sense." Indeed, the two elements can be separated historically: "The celestial ascent of the shaman is a survival, profoundly modified and sometimes degenerated, of the archaic religious ideology – centred on faith in a Celestial Supreme Being . . . the descent to Hell, the fight against evil spirits, and . . . the

increasingly familiar relations with spirits which aim at their incorporation or at the possession of the shaman by them, are all *inno-
vations.*" [11]

Thus, according to Eliade, we may discern two historically distinct strata or evolutionary stages: first the authentic *shamanistic
celestial ascent,* and second the subsidiary and diluting *possession
by spirits.* In company with many other writers on the subject,[12]
Eliade tends to associate the former "pure shamanism" (sometimes
called "white shamanism" in the literature) with prehistoric Siberian hunter-gatherers and so with paleolithic cave art. Pater Schmidt[13]
held precisely the opposite view, contending that primitive "black"
shamanism was associated with matriarchy and an agrarian mode
of production, and that the superior "white" shamanism, with its
stress on celestial flight, developed only at a later stage associated
with nomadism and patriarchy. Echoes of these evolutionary arguments recur today in the writing of Soviet specialists who, as V. N.
Basilov has observed, are bound to adopt a historical approach.

We shall return to these issues. For the moment our interest is in
examining the ways in which Eliade's antithesis between celestial
shamanic flight and spirit-possession has been elaborated and developed outside a historicist framework. Thus, disregarding its evolutionary overtones, the Belgian structuralist anthropologist Luc de
Heusch (1962) has sought to make this dichotomy between celestial
ascent and possession the springboard for an ingenious theory of
contrasting religious phenomena. Here shamanism is seen as an
"ascensual metaphysic" (a de-possession) and opposed to possession, which is seen as an incarnation. In line with Eliade, de Heusch
regards these as characteristic of different cosmologies and religions. He distinguishes between *involuntary possession* by evil spirits, which are *exorcised;* and *voluntary possession* by good spirits,
which are *incorporated.* The first he calls "inauthentic" possession,
the second "authentic." The same distinctions are applied to shamanism and a fourfold structural matrix proposed (Table 2).

Acknowledging criticism of the overrigidity of this schema, de
Heusch (1971) has since sought to trace transformations among
these various categories of religious phenomena; in fact, he has come
to see them as phenomenologically distinct types of trance. The
authentic shamanistic trance, in its Amerindian or Siberian forms,
de Heusch (1971: 270) asserts, "takes its position entirely in rela-

Table 2. *De Heusch's "geometry of the soul"*

Adorcism	Exorcism
Insertion of soul/spirit	Extraction of soul/spirit
Shamanism A	*Shamanism B*
Shaman restores soul to patient, i.e., cures "soul-loss."	Shaman extracts foreign pathogenic spirit.
Possession A: "authentic"	*Possession B: "inauthentic"*
Injection of a new soul/spirit	Extraction of foreign spirit

tion to therapy: the doctor is the general healer licensed in the course of – and by – trance. . . . The trance state is, for a true shaman, that in which he operates *in a hot state*, with hyper-lucid agitation." The authentic shaman for de Heusch is essentially "clairvoyant" and endowed with the "extraordinary facility of seeing the spirits, of discovering them, of knowing their secrets and with the power of exorcising them." The French ethnomusicologist Gilbert Rouget (1980) also accepts these distinctions, insisting (implausibly) that while all sorts of intermediate forms exist between shamanism and possession, the distinction nevertheless remains "fundamental."

In a series of collaborative studies culminating in a publication directed at a wide general readership, Erika Bourguignon (1976) has pursued a similar path, seeking correlations among different types of ecstatic states and different societies or social formations. Her point of departure is de Heusch's distinction between authentic and inauthentic possession, which she labels "positive" and "negative" respectively. Recognizing correctly that trance and possession are not necessarily identical, Bourguignon sees "possession" without trance (P) and possession with trance (PT) as opposed religious phenomena associated with different modes of social organization. The protean resources of G. P. Murdock's *Ethnographic Atlas* are employed to explore how societies where possession (P) occurs differ from those where possession-and-trance (PT) hold sway. The author finds statistical justification for the conclusion that "P societies are on the whole less complex than PT societies." "P societies," moreover, tend to engage in hunting, gathering, and fishing, whereas "PT societies" depend more heavily on agriculture and animal husbandry for subsistence. This contrast Bourguignon associates with child-rearing practices that encourage "self-reliance, independence, initiative and achievement motivation" in hunting and gathering (P) societies, but *not* in pastoral or agricultural (PT) societies. Since Bourguignon (1976: 44–9) apparently associates possession (rather than possession-trance) with shamanism, Eliade's ancient shamanic hunters seem here to be hovering in the background.

Although she is more systematic (if in a rather mechanical way) in her handling of comparative data, Bourguignon thus falls into the same trap as de Heusch, where she is joined inadvertently by Mary Douglas (1970). Douglas's attempts to handle the problems posed by shamanism and possession display the same basic fault – unjustified reification of cultural categories and religious and emotional phenomena. Douglas confidently assumes that whole societies (i.e., ethnic groups) can be graded in terms of degrees of positive or negative emotional attitudes toward possession. Thus in the case of the Nilotic-speaking peoples of the southern Sudan, she asserts (on the basis of Evans-Pritchard 1956), that the Nuer fear trance and regard it as dangerous. The neighboring Mandari (Buxton 1973) are even more terrified of spirit-possession. By contrast the Dinka, Douglas claims, welcome trance with open arms, valuing it as a positive, beneficent experience. These gradations in culturally stereotyped attitudes (reified by Douglas) are claimed to correlate with corresponding gradations in "group and grid," vague concepts that Douglas employs to describe the "hold" different societies exert on individual members.

In this "test case," Douglas considers the social organization of the Mandari to be much more tightly integrated, with stronger constraints on its individual members, than that of the Dinka, which is loosely structured. In her schema, the Nuer lie midway between these extremes. As she puts it, somewhat elliptically: "For the Mandari, group is strongest; for the Nuer group is weaker but grid is strongest; for the Dinka, grid and group are weaker than for the Nuer" (Douglas 1970: 96). As anyone familiar with the ethnographic evidence will appreciate, this impressionistic assessment of variations in the political organization of these three Nilotic peoples is highly questionable. In terms of formality of political organization and group cohesion, it would be more convincing to locate the Dinka as lying between the Nuer (the epitome of uncentralized egalitarianism) and the Mandari, who are after all organized in small chiefdoms.

We must not be sidetracked, however, into a discussion of what for Mary Douglas is merely illustrative ethnography. The basic idea here is that loosely structured conditions encourage trance and possession, whereas tightly integrated structures discourage these abandoned styles of religiosity. "The weaker the social constraints, the more bodily dissociation is approved and treated as a central ritual adjunct for channeling benign power to the community. The stronger the social pressures, the more magicality in ritual and in the definition of sin" (Douglas 1970: 97). More generally, according to the Durkheimian principle of "symbolic replication," religious feeling corresponds directly to the social conditions which, it is assumed, inspire it. We may note here that in line with the American culture and personality school of Whiting, Child, and others explicitly invoked by Bourguignon, Douglas implicitly assumes that undifferentiated emotional attitudes can be assigned to entire *societies* as though they were *individuals* with specific and predictable personalities. (It is thus unsurprising that Douglas should find direct parallels between the personalities of individuals and the "cosmologies" of societies.)

III

If it is in fact dubious whether stable attitudes toward emotive phenomena can be attributed even to individual personalities, it is certainly erroneous to imagine that in any meaningful sense whole cultures (so-called "societies") can be characterized as exhibiting "positive" or "negative" responses to trance and possession. Indeed, all the features that have been distinguished as signifying separate phenomena associated with contrasting social formations (past or present) actually regularly occur together within a single cultural context. This can be shown in various cultural settings; I shall take that of the Tungus as the model here. Anyone who takes the trouble to read carefully Shirokogoroff's masterpiece on Tungus shamanism, *The Psychomental Complex of the Tungus* (1935), will discover how superficial and simplistic are these other treatments of shamanism and possession. Like Bourguignon, the Tungus distinguish between possession (P) and possession-trance (PT), and also trance (T) without possession. So in Bourguignon's terms they are P, PT, and T all at once. Like de Heusch, they distinguish between desired and undesired possession by benign and evil forces. Thus these distinctions in attitudes towards trance and possession, which Douglas asserts to be typical of three different Nilotic societies, can all be found in the single cultural setting of the Tungus.

All these features, which others have seen as separate self-sustaining styles of religiosity, are in reality constituent elements in the composite shamanistic complex. Within this context (for they are not limited to it), the contrast that Bourguignon and de Heusch draw between negative and positive possession experiences corresponds regularly (although not exclusively) to serial phases in the assumption of the shamanistic career. Above all, *pace* de Heusch and Eliade, possession is not necessarily excluded by, or opposed to, shamanism. Let us return to Shirokogoroff (1935: 269), who tells us: "In all the Tungus languages the term (shaman) refers to persons of both sexes who have mastered spirits, who at their will can introduce these spirits into themselves and use their power over their spirits in their own interests, particularly helping other people who suffer from the spirits; in such a capacity they may possess a complex of special methods for dealing with the spirits." Often the shaman permanently incarnates these spirits (which may be those of his clan), which may manifest themselves when he is in a trance at a public seance – "shamanizing," as Shirokogoroff puts it. The shaman's body is a temple or tabernacle for the spirits, a vehicle or receptacle, what Shirokogoroff a little quaintly calls a "placing" and specifically differentiates from an icon.

This therapeutic vocation is typically announced by, and assumed, after a traumatic experience associated with hysteroid behavior interpreted as uncontrolled possession. "The shaman may begin his life career with a psychosis but cannot carry on his functions if he cannot master himself" (Shirokogoroff 1935: 366). The Tungus, Shirokogoroff stresses, distinguish between a person possessed by spirits and spirits possessed by the shaman. No one, he adds, is considered a shaman unless he can control spirits and introduce or expel them at will. At the beginning of his career he is supposed to have at least one spirit with whose help he can master other spirits. "No one can be accepted as a shaman unless he can demonstrably experience ecstasy – a half-delirious hysterical condition – 'abnormal' in European terms" (Shirokogoroff 1935: 274). This ecstatic state is achieved with the aid of a number of techniques: focusing the mind by staring fixedly into a brass mirror (which is regarded as a spirit "placing"); drumming and singing; inhaling of resinous smoke; drinking "a big cup of vodka"; smoking pipes of tobacco.[14] The spirits involved in this shamanistic seance, and more generally in the Tungus cosmology, cannot be simply classified as "good" or "bad" because (unlike Douglas, Bourguignon, and other ethnocentric anthropologists) the Tungus do not distinguish spirits in this unambiguous fashion. Any spirit, Shirokogoroff insists (1935: 121–22) may be malevolent, benevolent, or neutral, according to context and treatment, and more particularly depending on whether or not it is "mastered" by a shaman in relation to his local community.

Despite Eliade's emphasis on the theme of mystical flight to the "upper world," the Tungus, according to Shirokogoroff, actually place more stress on the shaman's spiritual voyages to the "lower world." More generally, he records that among all Tungus groups there are many occasions of shamanizing that are not concerned with either of these realms, but on the contrary with mastering spirits *in this world*. Examples cited include the liberation of a person from the spirits of a hostile shaman, or clan, or foreign spirits; the liberation of a clan from spirit attack; the expulsion of malevolent spirits and their mastering; sacrifice to benevolent or malevolent spirits; and divination of the causes of affliction with the aid of the shaman's auxiliary spirits. The essence of the shaman's role, Shirokogoroff insists, lies in his ability to incorporate potentially dangerous spirits into his own body, thus neutralizing or "mastering" them. This power to control spirits may, of course, be lost with age or in the competition with rival shamans; such judgments clearly reside with public opinion among the various Tungus clans. Although he notes exceptions, Shirokogoroff maintains that this ecstatic shaman who incarnates spirits typically differs from the elected clan priest, who is also designated by the word "shaman." Finally, we should note that at this time female shamans were almost as common as male shamans. This Shirokogoroff relates to what he considers an unusual degree of equality between the sexes among the Tungus. The general validity of Shirokogoroff's classical interpretation has been fully confirmed in the meticulous reexamination and masterly analysis of all the relevant Siberian ethnographic data by Anna-

Leena Siikala, to whose illuminating model of the shaman's role we shall return.[15]

Further afield, Carmen Blacker's study[16] of Japanese shamanism provides confirmation of this composite picture of what one might call "Ur-shamanism," including uncontrolled primary and controlled secondary phases of possession behavior, the coexistence of trance and possession – sometimes combined, sometimes separate – and the presence of out-of-body shamanistic experiences (mystical flight) and spirit-possession. In the syncretic (Shinto-Buddhistic) Japanese religious tradition, Blacker stresses the complementary roles of two religious figures. These are the spirit-inspired medium (*miko*), a vessel through whom spirits speak to mortals, and the ascetic shaman proper (*shamon*). The latter is primarily a healer whose soul ascends to the heavenly cosmos, or who makes this journey here on earth through what Blacker calls "symbolic mimesis" – climbing mountains that represent spiritual ascent. Like his Tungus counterpart, the Japanese shaman has helping spirits and can indeed also incarante spirits as well as sending his soul out on astral voyages. As Blacker (1975: 27) says, "Complementary though they may at first appear, the medium and the ascetic are closely bound together. Both must undergo the same ascetic practice before their particular kind of power can be acquired"; and "sometimes both kinds of power seem to be present, or at any rate overlapping, in the same person." In feudal Japan, "it was common to find . . . an ascetic husband married to a female medium."

Finally, to emphasize again how we may expect spirit-possession and shamanism, and possession and trance, to occur together in a single cultural setting, I cite Wazir-Jahan Karim's subtle analysis (1981) of shamanism among the Ma'Betisek aborigines of Malaysia. This careful study shows how the local term for shaman literally means a "person who becomes spirit-possessed." In the diagnostic healing seance, the shaman is possessed voluntarily by his "helping spirits" (introduced by the lordly Malay tiger spirits) and may or may not enter into a trance state. "The mental state of the performer whether in trance or not is not given much relevance; the state of spirit-possession is culturally explained by the audience according to set symptoms which appear in the seance. Trance-like states . . . are not an essential characteristic of a shamanistic seance" (Wazir-Jahan Karim 1981: 160). More generally, in certain con-

Table 3. *Interpretations of mystical experience*

Experience	Interpretation	Response
Bad, feared "Inauthentic," "negative"	Devil	Exorcism (cf. shock treatment)
Good, appreciated, "authentic," "positive"	God	Domestication (cf. psychoanalysis)

texts where it is unpredictable and uncontrolled, spirit-possession (associated with illness and madness) is avoided and feared, whereas in the shamanistic seance it is guided and controlled by the shaman.

IV

With these provisos and qualifications, we can now characterize the shaman as an inspired prophet and healer, a charismatic religious figure with the power to control the spirits, usually by incarnating them. If spirits speak through him, he is also likely to have the capacity to engage in mystical flight and other "out of body experiences."[17] As Shirokogoroff amply documented for the Tungus, fully appreciating the implications, an initial traumatic experience or illness interpreted as possession is typically the passport which, through progressive involvement with spirits, leads to the assumption of the role that Raymond Firth and others have identified as that of the medium, and which in its turn may lead to the more active and managerial role of shaman – master (or mistress) of spirits. Indeed, as Mircea Eliade himself rightly argues[18] – and demonstrates with an impressive wealth of ethnographic evidence – from the point of view of the shaman this is in fact the standard pattern of "shamanistic initiation."

De Heusch, Bourguignon, and Douglas, it will be recalled, assumed with some variations that the phenomenological (subjective) quality of a "mystical" experience unambiguously determined its evaluation in terms of the mystical force (or forces) to which it would be attributed and the corresponding ritual action or treatment (Table 3).

In reality, however, the initial experience is usually in essence

Table 4. *Episodic model of the ecstatic/shamanistic career*

Phase I	Phase II	Phase III
"Involuntary, uncontrolled, unsolicited" ⟶ possession (or other seizure, e.g., illness or other trauma)	Accommodated, domesticated ⟶	Controlled, voluntary, solicited trance
Patient ⟶		Healer

ambiguous or ambivalent and admits of two contrasting possible responses – exorcism (rejection) or domestication (acceptance, introjection, identification). In the latter case, the spirit or spirits responsible for the initial (and retrospectively initiatory) trauma are subsequently transformed into "helping spirits" by a process recalling that referred to by psychologists as "identifying with the aggressor." As I have already argued, these mystical encounters are *not* characteristic of different cultures, evolutionary stages, modes of production, and so forth, but regularly (although not invariably) coexist in a single cultural setting and period. Indeed, as Anna-Leena Siikala[19] shrewdly observes, such ostensibly diametrically opposed phenomena as pathogenic demonic possession and spirit-inspired shamanizing are, in practice, likely to be mutually reinforcing.

If we now expand the domestication (rather than exorcism) response, we can readily discern what is, I believe, the fundamental structure of shamanistic initiation. Here the initial traumatic experience signaling spiritual attention becomes a divine call, all the more impressive because its unsolicited, traumatic character establishes the bona fides of the new recruit as one forced by the overwhelming power of the spirits into their service. As the new devotee protests his or her unworthiness, so he or she establishes all the more securely the inevitability and authenticity of the "call." (Such striking declarations of shamanistic election repay close scrutiny.) Hence the shamanistic career is a true "cult of affliction," to use the term favored by V. Turner (1969), A. L. Siikala,[20] and myself (Lewis 1971: 66ff.).

This initiatory process (Table 4) includes at least three quite well-

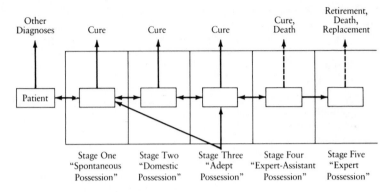

Figure 1. Paradigm of the individual possession career

defined Van Gennepian phases, episodes, or perhaps better "roles." For clarity of description and analysis we should distinguish such states or roles as carefully as possible. Trance and possession should not be confused, unless they coincide. At the same time we should recognize the limits of such classification and the confusion and distortion that excessive reification promotes. A rigid adherence to the term "spirit medium" because it seems safe, when shaman would be more appropriate, often serves to conceal rather than reveal significant common sociological features. In fact many – perhaps most – of those described in the ethnographic literature as "spirit mediums" (e.g., the Malaysian *bomoh* or modern Western spirit medium) have spirit familiars at their command. It is with the aid of these "spirit guides" that in seance contexts they diagnose and resolve the problems of their clients. They are thus "masters of spirits" and so shamans.[21] It must of course be understood, as Shirokogoroff demonstrates, that shamans can also *lose* their mastery over spirits and risk relapsing, in terms of our model, into the role of patient.

This regression is linked to the judgment that powers once controlled for the protection and benefit of the community are now unleashed to threaten the well-being of the group. Mastery of the spirits remains ultimately provisional, and the shaman whose powers are judged to be waning, perhaps in competition with new aspirants, readily becomes a target for witchcraft accusations – which as we have seen may include charges of cannibalism. Our episodic processual model thus serves to clarify the assumption, abuse, and

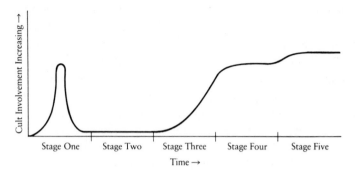

Figure 2. The possession career in relation to cult involvement

loss of shamanic authority; it also emphasizes the volatility, permeability, and reversability of these roles. This is why individually the terms *possessed person, spirit medium,* and *shaman* are not very helpful typologically at the cultic or cultural level. Indeed, our tripartite model stressing how these states overlap and flow together is probably too condensed and abbreviated; it should be expanded into a fuller paradigm of the "possession career," as indicated in Figures 1 and 2 (after Alice Morton, 1973). This five-stage schema traces the sequence of possession contexts from the initial, spontaneously possessed patient stage to that of professional expert-healer. Potential drop-out from further possession cult involvement is available at each stage through "cures" that remove the individual from the cycle of spirit-possession.

To the extent that they frequently recapitulate the shaman's own initiatory experiences, these various roles may also be actualized in the context of the seance. Here the shaman regularly appears as possessed by spirits, acts as their vocal medium, and conspicuously masters them. As Shirokogoroff fully appreciated and as the French surrealist poet and ethnographer Michel Leiris (1958) has sensitively demonstrated for Ethiopian possession and shamanism, the shamanistic seance is high theater.[22] The shaman does not merely act or perform, but rather assumes and enacts with full ecstatic virtuosity what Anna-Leena Siikala calls his "counter-roles" – the materializations of his spirit guides. He moves in and out of a series of trance states of varying intensity, but rarely loses contact with his audience (however oblivious he may seem).

If the seance provides the natural setting for the enactment of the shaman's richly stored repertoire of roles, shamanism itself seems best defined along the lines indicated by the Russian scholar V. N. Basilov[23] – "a cult whose central idea is the belief in the ability of some individuals chosen by some spirits to communicate with them while in a state of ecstasy and perform the functions of an intermediary between the world of spirits and the given human collective (collectivity)." Although there is much to be said for it, this view does not necessarily entail unreservedly endorsing the belief of Basilov and other Soviet specialists that shamanism is essentially a "pre-class" religion that may nevertheless survive in class societies in a marginal, peripheral cult form. It does not matter how the balance between possession and soul-flight is pitched, whether or not a three-tier cosmology is present (though often it is), nor whether Vivianne Paques's (1964) "cosmic tree" is part of the picture (though often it is). These and many other symbolic motifs are widely if not universally associated with shamanism. There are many local variations in cosmology that are not intrinsically linked to shamanism. As Shirokogoroff himself constantly emphasizes, Tungus religion and cosmology are not static phenomena – historically and geographically they have been influenced by culture borrowing and exchange on a wide front, with the shaman playing a crucial innovative role as receiving agent and mediator for alien spiritual forces. There is abundant evidence of significant external influence from Chinese, Manchu, and Buriat, to say nothing of Russian, sources. Buddhism also seems to have played a powerful role in shaping Tungus religion, although by the second decade of this century the majority of the population had become "nominal" Christians, according to Shirokogoroff. Syncretism remained the order of the day; the Russian St. Nicholas had been adopted by the Tungus as the "grand master" of shamans. There is a remarkable correspondence between this protean figure and our contemporary European and North American image of Santa Claus, flying through the skies with his reindeer-drawn sleigh, laden with miraculous gifts.

Such homely allusions will not, I trust, distract the reader from the central intention of this chapter, which by applying a processural, developmental model seeks to elucidate the concept "shaman," restoring it to its proper context in the possession career. This exercise in unpacking an ethnically specific term for what is actually the very epitome of charismatic authority may, it is hoped, contribute to a more informed understanding of universal religious roles, which for too long have been treated as though they represented different species beyond the reach of effective comparative analysis.

6

The power of the past: African "survivals" in Islam

I

If the shaman triumphantly conquers and domesticates malign power and transmutes it into benign mystical energy (converting negative into positive charisma), his heroic role may still be exercised in a cult context, which in its wider external setting remains marginal and retains its negative aura of witchcraft and cannibalism. Marginality may be traced either spatially or temporally, and the two dimensions, as we shall see, are apt to interpenetrate and coalesce. This concluding chapter will argue that, in addition to providing a deeper and more accurate understanding of the *internal* dynamics of charismatic cults, our comparative analysis also illuminates the *external* significance of cults in the definition of ideological boundaries. Reconsidering in this wider context some of the cults discussed earlier, we thus achieve new insight into the meaning of "survivals" in religion (and of religious orthodoxy), taking the particular circumstances of African Islam to exemplify more general phenomena in world religions.

As with other world religions, elements of belief and practice that in a given Muslim setting are not officially recognized as part of international orthodoxy are generally assumed to represent local "survivals" from pre-Islamic times. Such assumptions about the persistence of unwelcome archaic elements from the past are by no means limited to the traditional religious elite. They are equally readily endorsed by modern scholars of religion. A characteristic example of this widespread view is found in a contemporary account of Tunisian popular Islam entitled "Survivances mystiques et culte de possession dans le maraboutisme Tunisien." The author, a Tunisian sociologist, presents maraboutism (the north African cult of saints and holy men) as the embodiment of two "systems of different values: asceticism and animism."[1] Maraboutism, we are told, derives from pre-Islamic north African roots, and its associated cult of possession is the means by which "ancient animist beliefs are perpetuated. . . . In contact with Islam, the traditional 'spirits' are simply confounded with Muslim jinns and the veneration paid to sorcerers transferred to saints *awliya"* (Ferchiou: 48).

This interpretation, which ascribes pluralist tendencies in the contemporary practice of popular Islam to the pre-Islamic past, is naturally reinforced by those perennial currents of Islamic fundamentalism (recurrently manifested as "reformism") that condemn without qualification all forms of saintly mediation as heresy. At different times and places most Muslim cultures strongly suffused with mystical Sufism have not lacked for stern critics preaching such alternative Islamic fundamentalism. This antimystical puritanism has, in turn, fostered down-to-earth skepticism about the exaggerated powers attributed by the credulous to certain saints. If refined literary Sufism attracts these strictures, the florid possession cults readily seen as its vulgar popular expression invite violent denunciation as stubborn relics of "pre-Islamic superstition," such as might be found among recently converted pagans on the fringes of the House of Islam.

Puritan orthodoxy – or "scripturalism," as it is sometimes misleadingly called – and Sufi mysticism clearly represent diametrically different styles of Islamic religiosity. Do they then possess equally distinct social correlates? Western writers on Islam often assume so, this view being perhaps most trenchantly formulated in Ernest Gellner's "pendulum model" of Islam.[2] According to this theory, these styles reflect the theological chasm separating the literate well-informed *'ulama* (Muslim clerics) of the towns and their illiterate (or semiliterate) country cousins. The distinction follows the familiar contrast between "great" and "little" traditions emphasized so often in discussions of the other "world religions."

This interpretation seems to me inadequate. In its most basic terms, what is really at stake here is a broader issue: the fierce and constantly recharged theological debate concerning the interpretation of the Prophet's message. Here attention focuses on the meaning and importance of such famous revelatory passages in the Koran as the injunction to believers to "seek the means to come to Him" (v.

39), traditionally taken by Sufis to signal the mediatory power of saints. As the distinguished Arabist A. J. Arberry sums the matter up, in the history of Islam "the esoteric exposition of the Koran became a central point in the hard training of the Sufi."[3] In such circumstances rustic illiteracy could hardly be expected to be the necessary precondition for developing a Sufistic interpretation of Islam; indeed, rather the contrary. At the same time, what fundamentalist theologians, and their unconscious sociological hagiologists, stereotypically represent as potentially heretical and certainly marginal − superstitious "pre-Islamic survivals" − possess a highly problematic quality. As I hope to demonstrate, phenomena characterized as "fringe" or "marginal" Islam are, on closer inspection, sometimes so intimately connected with "core" Islam that they seem part of a single complex. Morevoer, what in a particular cultural context is regularly categorized as "pre-Islamic survival" is in many cases nothing of the sort.

II

The concept of "pre-Islamic survivals" is naturally consistent with a historical (not to say evolutionary) approach and is part of the well-documented process by which today's religion (or ideology) reduces yesterday's religion to the status of magic, each successive religious vogue marginalizing its predecessor. While this process obviously does take place, we have also to recall the alternative possibility in such religious dialogues − the synthesis or syncretism exemplified among the Bedouin Arabs themselves[4] and among other "tribal" Islamic peoples (e.g., the Somali)[5] in the transformation of local and clan ancestors into Sufi saints. In the Muslim world generally, pilgrimages to the shrines of such local saints are usually known as the "poor man's *hajj*," thus making a direct equation with pilgrimage to Mecca. Both processes (marginalization and syncretism) may occur at the same time − some elements of an earlier religion being marginalized (as evil *jinns* or sorcery, *sihir*) while others are assimilated as saints. As our earlier discussion suggests (Chapter 3), spirit-possession cults in Islamic cultures provide a convenient and revealing context for examining these various possible accommodations.

Such cults are regularly presented as being based upon pre-Islamic survivals. Thus the famous West African *bori* cult (Chapter 2) is generally treated in the literature as representing the religion of the pre-Islamic Hausa, displaced by Islam and thrust into a shadowy, peripheral position in a male-dominated Muslim society.[6] A similar pattern emerges with greater clarity in the case of the formerly matrilineal Zaramo of Tanzania, where the adoption of Islam has apparently weakened the position of women, who seek redress through possession cults involving traditional (as well as modern) spirits.[7]

Although these cults tend to be presented negatively in the Islamic settings where they flourish and to appeal particularly to women, low status men, and marginal people generally, their position is fundamentally ambiguous. Some at least of the spirits involved are readily subsumed under those mentioned in the Koran and so are scripturally legitimated; others are even considered to be Muslim. Again, although the rituals associated with them are regularly described in the literature as "exorcisms," the adequacy and accuracy of this characterization can be questioned since treatment frequently entails recurrent rituals and in effect initiation into specialized cults (cf. Chapter 5). What is really involved is, in fact, often a kind of conversion.

Recognition of this crucial fact opens the door to a deeper understanding of the problem of syncretism and survival in African Islam (and no doubt in Islam elsewhere as well). The standard approach to the dissemination of Islam in Africa follows the classic diffusionist model, whose three stages are described by the leading British authority, J. S. Trimingham,[8] as "germination," "crisis," and "gradual reorientation." From a similar but more specifically theological perspective, H. J. Fisher[9] has recently proposed an analogous Van Gennepian tripartite formula involving "quarantine," "mixing," and "reform."

III

Although such cultural diffusion models are clearly valuable, it is also important to examine how socioeconomic changes create conditions favoring the adoption of Islam (and in other contexts, the other "world religions").[10] A critical consideration here is the scope that Islam offers as a viable personal and universalistic group identity when socioeconomic changes are expanding social and experiential horizons.

In this context, the flamboyant, ecstatic conversion experience of which so much is made in Christianity (both historically and currently, in charismatic circles) has, I believe, been overlooked in Islam – or at least in African Islam, where a number of suggestive cases have been reported. In west Africa, for example, among the Mossi who are in the process of becoming Muslims, barrenness in pagan women may be diagnosed by diviners as a sign that potential children refuse to be born except as Muslims. Conversion to Islam is the obvious remedy (Skinner 1966: 360).

This "therapeutic" route to the faith is certainly in evidence among the Giriama of Kenya, traditionally subsistence cultivators trading with the Muslim Swahili and Arabs of the east African coast. Beginning in the 1920s, as they began to emulate their neighbors in producing cash crops, a new entrepreneurial class came into existence among this people. These successful traders attracted the envy of their less well-favoured kinsmen and were evidently "in the market" for protection against such mystical aggression. Some found asylum by adopting Christianity (in the spirit of the Protestant ethic, according to Weber and Tawney); others became Muslims. The way in which this happened is quite apposite: Members of this nascent class fell victim to illnesses that were diagnosed as caused by Muslim spirits for which the only secure remedy was conversion to Islam. Such "therapeutic Muslims" had, of course, been called to Islam, involuntarily, by an illness for which they could not be held accountable. They had not sought this; it had happened against their will. But the consequences are revealing. The adoption of Islam, with its various dietary requirements, freed these upwardly mobile privileged individuals from certain traditional communal obligations. At the same time, it protected them against mystical attack and provided them with the higher status Swahili-style Islamic identity that suited their economic activities and ambitions.[11]

This appeal of Muslim therapeutic techniques, and indeed of Islam itself as a mystical defense system has, I think, been underestimated in analyzing the expansion of Islam in sub-Saharan Africa. In the present context, however, my concern is to emphasize how Muslims may be recruited by a process which in other circumstances would smack of unorthodox deviance or of flamboyant fringe maraboutism. An even more instructive if more complex case, perhaps, is the cult of Sheikh Hussein of Bale in southern Ethiopia. Sheikh Hussein, whose origins appear to go back to the thirteenth century and who is thus, in effect, the spiritual residue of the ancient Muslim state of Bale, has become in effect the patron saint of Muslims in Ethiopia. The annual festival at the shrine attracts great numbers of pilgrims from places as far distant as northern and central Ethiopia, northern Kenya, and southern Somalia. Sheikh Hussein has connections with the Somali coast and, more generally, with the inter-riverine area of southern Somalia, where an elaborate complex of shrines dedicated to the saint replicates the parent pilgrim center in Bale.[12]

In its contemporary form in Bale, where there has been a complex succession of ethnic migrations over the centuries, this Islamic cult has come to embody prominent features from the traditional religion of the Oromo peoples who invaded the region in the sixteenth century. The Oromo, it must be appreciated, are Cushitic speakers like the Somali, to whom they are closely related ethnically and historically. Sheikh Hussein's cult has thus been to a degree "Oromo-ised" by the accretion of cultural elements that are *post-* rather than *pre-*Islamic. Indeed its constituent elements have been successively de- and re-Islamicized in what is by no means a unique process in the history of such religious movements. As has long been recognized, the cult's wide-ranging appeal in an Ethiopia dominated by Semitic-speaking Christians owes much to this syncretic character, blending Islamic and Oromo symbols and projecting an Islamic identity that today subsumes and transmutes traditional Oromo values on a pattern influenced by the Somali Muslim prototype.

This synthetic Muslim identity has assumed a pervasive spiritual character that extends far beyond Sheikh Hussein's shrine and those who make pilgrimages there. In northern Kenya, where it has penetrated widely (apparently quite recently), Sheikh Hussein's cult has assumed an active missionary role in the form, as its devotees see it, of a Sufi mystical religious order known as Husseiniya. In the small township of Isiolo, with its ethnically mixed Cushitic and Nilo-Hamitic population, in competition with Christianity the Sheikh's cult is especially prominent among the local Cushitic groups. Recruitment to the "brotherhood" frequently follows illness and affliction, treated by initiation into the syncretic cult and the adoption or confirmation of Islamic identity. Membership appeals particularly to "poor, destitute Borana (a branch of the Oromo) and

Somali" – especially destitute pastoralists who have lost their live-
stock in war and famine and drifted into Isiolo district headquarters
seeking a means of survival (Hjort 1979: 42). There are a higher
proportion of Borana (Oromo) men than Somali men in the cult,
which despite its Somali connections in Ethiopia is viewed by the
local Somali Islamic establishment in northern Kenya as "primitive" and "satanic" – a kind of intrusive spiritual malaise "picked
up from the bush." Cult adherents are even forbidden to enter the
mosque. This negative view is shared by the Kenyan administrative
authorities, who apparently regard the flamboyant popular rituals
as encouraging political and social discontent – to which, in all
probability, the rites are actually a harmless, palliative reaction.
Sternly condemned in the mosque by the orthodox Somali sheikhs
(usually members of the Qadariya or Salihiya religious orders), the
cult is nevertheless warmly supported by their wives. This is an
interesting but by no means unusual example of sex-linked religious
pluralism with close analogies to the Tunisian situation, to which
we shall return presently. For the moment, however, let us simply
note here that what the women embrace and the men discard as
"pre-Islamic superstition" is something much more complicated than
this dismissive categorization implies.

IV

In southern Somalia, to which we now turn, Sheikh Hussein's cult
exists alongside the more pervasive and widely known *zar* cult (*sar*
in Somali),[13] which we have already encountered in Chapter 3. If,
in this context, the Husseiniya might tendentiously be claimed to
subsume local pre-Islamic "survivals" (inasmuch as there is a pre-
Islamic Oromo ethnic substratum in the population of southern
Somalia), this is emphatically out of the question with regard to the
sar possession cult. In its Somali form, there is no evidence that the
word *sar* refers to a local pre-Islamic spirit or ritual. On the contrary, the term conveys the idea of extraneous or external origin
and is associated with Ethiopia, whence what is generally considered the most dangerous variety of spirit intrusion (*mengis,* from
Amharic "government") clearly derives.[14] As we have seen in Chapter
2, there is a striking prevalence of women victims, which has generally been interpreted as reflecting the frustrations associated with
their subordinate position in a male-dominated culture.[15]

As we can now see more clearly than before, the *sar* possession cult among Somali women is primarily an urban rather than a rural phenomenon. Although men are the dominant sex in the social system of Somali pastoral nomads, women, charged with the management of small stock, enjoy considerable freedom and never wear the veil. It is only in towns that women are sometimes seen veiled,[16] and it is precisely in such urban contexts that possession flourishes. This contrast fits neatly with the male accusation that the spirits – which men are apt to condemn and regard skeptically – attack the wives of the rich more often than those of the poor, treatment being an expensive business and typically adding (as we have seen) to the afflicted wife's wardrobe of costly clothes and personal jewelry. Although the exploited husbands denounce the cult as "primitive superstition," it is striking that the women most deeply involved are actually not hard-pressed nomads of the bush but, on the contrary, relatively prosperous members of the new urban population, wearing modern dresses and living in homes, equipped, in addition to servants, with radios, tape recorders, and refrigerators.[17] Perhaps the most severe frustration for those who have not yet been liberated in a modern sense, through education and extra-domestic employment, is boredom.

A recent study of the incidence of cases interpreted in the same *zar* idiom in Egypt is revealing in this respect.[18] In the intensively cultivated Nile Delta, *zar* cult involvement is more prominent in the lives of rich village leaders and landowners than in those of poor *fellahin* peasants. This is directly linked to constraints imposed by Islamic respectability on well-to-do wives, who are more homebound and dependent than their peasant counterparts. The latter enjoy greater economic and domestic independence, more freedom of movement, and stronger kin support. The richer women are more confined and cut off and correspondingly more intensely involved in expensive *zar* cult rituals, which their husbands pay for. Whatever cross-sexual tensions may be ventilated here, there is also a significant element of conspicuous consumption, as wives test and demonstrate the resources of their spouses (cf. Wilson 1967). Peasant women tend to be only occasionally attacked by *zar* spirits, at times of exceptional strain and difficulty, and are less likely to be drawn into formal cult membership and long-term (i.e., perpetual) cult activity.

The pattern in the neighboring Sudan is similar.[19] *Zar*, which as usual is viewed as an intrusive foreign influence, is essentially an urban bourgeois phenomenon, ensconced in the bosom of respectable, traditionalist Muslim families. At the upper end of the spirit catchment many of the women involved are married to prominent men, including religious dignitaries, who while denouncing *zar* as pagan idolatory are not above asking their wives to consult the cult leaders on their behalf. Again we find that the most keen adherents are women with rich husbands – prosperous merchants, butchers, contractors, goldsmiths. And, notwithstanding the controversy it evokes, *zar* programs have been staged on Sudanese television.

While some of the terminology employed in the rituals of this Sudanese women's *zar* cult directly parallels that used in marriage ceremonies, it is difficult not to be struck by the obvious similarities between this women's movement and the men's Sufi brotherhoods. Like the *tariqas*, the *zar* groups celebrate all the major Islamic festivals, and no rituals are held in the month of Ramadan. They begin and end their proceedings with prayers in honor of the Prophet Muhammad; their leaders,[20] who regularly go on pilgrimages to Mecca, are called *sheikhas* (female sheikhs) and like their male Sufi counterparts are said "to know the way" (that the faithful should follow). In both cases, the position of leader may be ascribed (by birth) or achieved (by initiation). Again, in the Sufi rituals men achieve states of ecstasy which (even if they differ in style and tempo) invite comparison to the women's possession trances in the *zar* cult.

The Sudanese pantheon of *zar* spirits, moreover, is headed by the "holy saints" – the founders of the brotherhoods traditionally so important in the lives of men. These are followed by other groups: the "Ethiopians"; the "Pashas"; the "Arabs" (representative of the nomadic Sudanese tribes); the "Europeans and Christians" – including Jews, Copts, Greeks, Armenians, French, and British (specifically General Gordon and Lord Cromer); the "ladies or daughters," associated with the prestigious "holy saints"; the "blacks" (from the south); the Fellata; and various other categories. These constitute loose general categories that readily admit new accretions. Thus for a time socialist soldier spirits made their appearance, and more recently Gamal Abdel Nasser and the Saudi OPEC oil minister Sheik Yamani are reported to have entered the

seance galaxy.[21] The *zar* spirit repertoire is evidently a fluid historical mirror of the world of male Sudanese experience.

V

While certain notorious non-Islamic historical figures – such as
General Gordon and Lord Cromer – thus appear to have had
immortality thrust upon them, in general the historical identity of
the spirits involved clearly makes it difficult to classify this Sudanese
possession cult as a straightforward survival or local pre-Islamic
phenomena. The same objection is obviously even more pertinent
when we consider the wider geographical distribution of the *zar*
cult along the east Africal litoral (and islands), in Egypt, North Africa,
and along the Arabian peninsula to Iran. Although sometimes known
under other names, throughout this vast area the cult retains its
Ethiopian associations and attracts women generally, along with
peripheral male immigrants from Somalia and the east African coast
who are treated as second-class citizens by those Arabian and Iranian employers whom they serve, often in low-status occupations.
As with its Sudanese version, this complex of possession cults
involving Muslim and non-Muslim spirits, holy men, and pagans,
seems generally to attract women of higher social position than its
male adherents.[22] This is consistent with the more strict segregation
of women in orthodox bourgeois circles, as noted earlier in relation
to the Egyptian *fellahin*.

Although possibly in some places subsuming other genuinely
indigenous local spirits[23] ("authentic survivals"), it is generally
accepted that the *zar* cult has spread by diffusion from Ethiopia.
This process is assumed to have accompanied the slave trade from
Ethiopia and the east African coast in the late eighteenth and early
nineteenth centuries and the subsequent settlement in the Arabian
peninsula of African migrant workers. Indeed, the evidence currently available suggests that *zar* only began to assume prominence
in Egypt in the second half of the nineteenth century, or even later.[24]

More generally, it appears that it was in this relatively recent
period that *zar* spirits began to diffuse widely outside their spiritual
headquarters (if not homeland) in the Gondar region of Ethiopia,
where they possessed both Christian and Muslim Ethiopians. Gondar is historically the center of Christian Ethiopia and of the fusion

between its Cushitic and Semitic cultures and religions. Its ecumenical spiritual pantheon thus also directly reflects this complex legacy, and it is striking to note that in this official bastion of Ethiopian Christendom the Arabic word "saint" (*weli*) is used interchangeably with the Amharic *zar,* and the leaders of *zar* cult groups are frequently referred to as "masters" (*bala*) of "saints" (*awliya*).

By analogy with other comparable "peripheral spirit cults" (see Chapter 2), it would probably be more accurate to speak of the diffusion (and rediffusion) of *zar* spirits rather than of an undifferentiated *zar* cult.[25] The dispersal of the spirits would then presumably be associated with increasingly intensive relations between the countries and peoples of the Nile and the horn of Africa during the Anglo-Egyptian administration of the Sudan and the ensuing *mahdiya* – at which time, Michel Leiris's informants in Gondar recalled,[26] a new class of militant Tigrean spirits known as *kabere* (from *keber,* pride, honor) began to possess people. This is surely also what the presence of the Pashas and of General Gordon and Lord Cromer in the Sudanese *zar* pantheon suggests. It is equally in accord with Leiris's observation that in Gondar one is especially likely to catch (or be caught by) *zar* through a chance encounter with a possessed person in a market. The pilgrimage to Mecca (whither the *zar* cult was also carried) was doubtless also a major vehicle in the wider spread of these, and many other, concepts and ideas.

However, the demonstration of effective connections and lines of communication for the potential spread of ideas (and cult practices) does not explain why they arose in their particular places of origin when they did, nor why they appealed to other sections of society in the centers to which they were carried. The latter explanation is to be found, I believe, as suggested earlier, in the special circumstances of those most prone to the attentions of these intrusive spirits. Frequently those concerned are marginal male migrants of non-Arab origin, and more generally, Muslim women – especially where an intensification of conservative orthodoxy further weakens the position and rights of women.[27]

It is tempting to speculate that the wider dissemination of *zar* in and from Ethiopia in the nineteenth century might be connected with the expansion and consolidation of the Christian Amhara empire under Menelik during this period. (This would be in harmony with the militaristic character attributed in Gondar to the *zar* spirits and with the emphasis placed on hunting and fighting motifs in the cult imagery). Beyond that, while discounting the "demonstration effect" as a necessary and sufficient explanation for the *diffusion* of new ideas, I do not think we should entirely ignore the factor of fashion. This again is clearly linked to the question of identity and status and to the manner in which perennial aspirations are aired and expressed.

It is unnecessary to discuss the parallel and, in north Africa, sometimes overlapping *bori* cult in comparable detail (see Chapter 2). Certainly its diffusion from its native northern Nigeria and Nigere is directly associated with the trans-Saharan slave trade and with African settlement amongst the local Arab and Berber populations of the Magreb. Even without such population movements, the trans-Saharan trading connections could well have prompted the influx of intrusive *bori* spirits to Islamic north Africa. Be that as it may, and whatever its original status amongst the Hausa, the fact is that in Arab north Africa the *bori* cult is obviously no more a bona fide pre-Islamic "survival" than its *zar* counterpart. It is thus highly appropriate that we should find references to *bori* spirits in Sudanese *zar* contexts (where the two words are sometimes used interchangeably), and to *zar* spirits in north African *bori* contexts. It is typical and equally apposite that the ambiguous possession cult siren Lalla "Aisha,"[28] who figures prominently in both regions, should be known in the Sudan as "the Maghrebi" and in Morocco as "the Sudani"! The traffic in spirits is almost as widespread and intensive as the teaching of Islam.

VI

With the examples of the *zar* and *bori* cults I have sought to demonstrate that, in the settings in which they flourish, these are far from representing genuine pre-Islamic "survivals." If, as in some cases they and their analogues may be, they are somewhere ultimately of pre-Islamic origin, then what we find here is a continuous process of reactive counterdiffusion; as the spirit of Islam flows in one direction, other spirits return the compliment, as it were. So religious phenomena that existed before Islam entered a given region, and which are there authentically "pre-Islamic," become after their diffusion to other Islamic areas post- and sometimes even pan-Islamic.

Religious currents in the Islamic metropolis are thus in constant dynamic tension with those on the periphery.[29]

Hence, although orthodox fundamentalist Islam stands at one end of the spectrum, with magical maraboutism at the other, these opposed religious styles cannot be unambiguously identified with the dichotomies between town and tribe, literate and illiterate, and so on. The first, if it does not actually entail at least tends to provoke the second as a supplement and appendix. It is not just that the marginal ritual practices of women mirror the men's saints' cult, there being as Sophie Ferchiou (1972: 48–64) puts it a distinctive male and female religious "comportment" in Islam. More is involved than simply a restrained male style of religiosity counterpoised by a flamboyant female mode. The burden of religious orthodoxy is depicted as falling primarily to men as the pilgrims and pillars of Islam, whose religious devotions count also for their womenfolk, who are thereby exempted from an equivalent degree of direct religiosity. From this perspective, with their Islamic embroidery, the women's possession cults seem to represent a kind of vicarious participation in the male-dominated Islamic sanctuary. My own alternative perspective suggests that the ecstatic women's cults have a direct appeal precisely to the wives of the more orthodox men – the models of Islamic respectability – while indirectly offering the latter the privilege of vicarious participation in what they ostensibly condemn as superstition and heresy. Thus, if there is a dual spiritual economy, its two branches are interdependent and complementary.

More generally, sociologists of Islam regularly attack Arabists and Orientalists for taking Islam literally, as it is presented in the Koran, rather than as it is expressed in the beliefs of living Muslims who interpret the Koran as they see fit. They, however, are also prone to present the "big tradition" view of Islam as the "religion of the book," treating supposed deviations as manifestations of rustic illiteracy and ignorance. This ignores the striking fact that the vast corpus of written sayings attributed to the Prophet (*hadith*) and interpretations broadcast from urban centers of Muslim excellence is regularly accompanied by an equally extensive *written* apparatus of magical and astrological Islamic lore. The latter not only provides an Islamic base and legitimation for local pre-Islamic mystical beliefs and rituals but actually sometimes introduces such "magical" beliefs where they did not previously exist. Indeed, as has recently been observed in Malaysia, "a growing Islamic fervour is equally balanced by an increasing interest in magic" (Wazir-Jahan Karim 1981: 204).

It is important to establish what is happening here. It is not just oral, pre-Islamic culture that dilutes the unswerving eternal truths conserved in literate mainstream Islam. Elements in literate mainstream Islam also introduce and perpetuate alternative renderings of the Prophet's message. Islam is thus not the "religion of the book" but, rather, the "religion of the books," a package of written compendia that in their catholic profusion facilitate the diffusion and rediffusion of so-called pre-Islamic survivals.

This reappraisal of the meaning of the concept of "survival" in the context of a world religion emphasizes once again the importance of accurately contextualizing beliefs, which was stressed in the opening chapter. The official picture of what does and does not constitute ideological orthodoxy is the officially constructed picture, molding and remolding the "past" to provide an effective backdrop for the revealed truth of the present. In this process the invention of antitradition is just as important as the invention of tradition. Thus what in terms of establishment values is marginal to society, and correspondingly charged with ambiguous negative power, becomes marginal in time – an anachronistic survival from the past.

The sinister power of the past attributed to these marginal cults of affliction generally, and particularized in the person of the shaman, includes dark allusions to witchcraft and cannibalism. Religious survivals, in the shape of marginal charismatic cults, thus bring together all those outwardly negative facets of mystical power that I have been arguing in this book are better understood as permutations of the same underlying phenomenon than as autonomous "things." Religious phenomena, of course, lend themselves exceedingly well to reification; and one of the main obstacles to progress here is the reluctance of so many anthropologists to submit such material to searching, empirically grounded analysis along the lines proposed in this book.

Notes

Chapter 1: Anthropological fieldwork and the context of belief
1. See the pamphlet *Department of Anthropology 1972–73* (London School of Economics, 1972), p. 4.
2. For an interesting analysis of the first edition of this British anthropologists' *Who's Who*, see E. and S. Ardener (1965: 295–314).
3. See, for example, E. Leach (1970).
4. C. Lévi-Strauss (1977, vol. 1: 328).
5. C. Lévi-Strauss (1977, vol. 1: 332).
6. C. Lévi-Strauss (1977, vol. 1: 337).
7. See Audrey Richards (1967: 286–98).
8. M. Mead (1972: 121).
9. Rosemary Firth (1972: 10–32).
10. See, e.g., J. B. Casagrande, ed. (1960: xi); C. Lévi-Strauss (1977, vol. 1: 373); and M. Freilich, ed. (1970: 13). In Freilich (1970) see also p. 35, where it is recommended that preparation for fieldwork include some training in psychotherapy.
11. Rosemary Firth (1972: 31).
12. E. E. Evans-Pritchard (1951: 77–9).
13. See, e.g., J. B. Casagrande (1960: xi), and M. Freilich (1970: 13), and for an admirably comprehensive recent discussion R. F. Ellen (1984).
14. For this analogy I owe much to conversations with Dr. Peter Fry, who I think perceived the parallel before I did.
15. It is thus not surprising that so many of those who write in this vein are Americans.
16. See, e.g., the very revealing final volume of the monumental *Mythologiques*, *L'Homme nu* (C. Lévi-Strauss 1971), particularly pp. 559–621.
17. Robert Murphy (1972: 24).
18. We must notice, however, that Lowie himself explains in the preface to the 1937 edition of *Primitive Society* (first edition: 1920) that he intended the phrase to convey his own disillusionment with Western civilization in the wake of the First World War.

19. Especially in those articles republished as the first part of *Anthropologie structurale*.
20. See A. Forge (1972).
21. Max Gluckman (1963: 35).
22. W. E. H. Stanner, in J. B. Casagrande (1960: 85).
23. V. W. Turner (1960: 335–37).
24. M. Griaule (1965: 220). For a perceptive recent "Anglophone" assessment of Griaule's contribution, see J. Clifford (1983: 121–56).
25. C. Lévi-Strauss (1970: 13).
26. M. Douglas (1957: 46–57). The anomalous fact that there are *two* Lele pangolins, only one of which is the object of a cult, seems to be disregarded in Professor Douglas's subsequent publications.
27. V. W. Turner (1967: 13).
28. E. E. Evans-Pritchard (1965: 24–7).
29. Raymond Firth (1960: 17).
30. Godfrey Lienhardt (1961).
31. M. Griaule (1965: 37).
32. A. Kiev (1972: 171–2).
33. See, e.g., K. Thomas (1971) and A. Macfarlane (1970).
34. E. E. Evans-Pritchard (1937).
35. I. M. Lewis (1971).
36. This interpretation goes back at least as far as C. Kluckhohn's *Navaho Witchcraft* (1944) and is echoed in such recent surveys as Lucy Mair (1969) and Charles Harrington and J. W. M. Whiting (1972: 469–508). Cf. also M. Marwick (1970: 280–95).
37. E. Leach (1966: 39–50). See also M. E. Spiro (1968: 242–61) and correspondence in *Man* (1968: 311–13, 651–6; 1969: 132–34).
38. Raymond Firth (1966: 1–17) and E. E. Evans-Pritchard (1966: 398). See also E. E. Evans-Pritchard (1956) and James Littlejohn (1970: 91–114).
39. Not, however, in my view for the reasons advanced in Rodney Needham's distillation of the opinions of the Oxford linguistic philosophers (Needham 1972). I find Ernest Gellner's "Concepts and Society" (1962) more helpful in diagnosing the anthropologist's obsessional tendency to treat all exotic beliefs as equally coherent and cogent, thus making it difficult to recognize significant inconsistencies. See also Gustav Jahoda's very interesting comments on some of the issues involved here from the standpoint of a social psychologist (Jahoda [1970a: 33–50]). See also Jahoda (1970b: 115–30; 1971).
40. See Mary Douglas (1970).
41. See Gilbert A. Lewis (1975). Dr. Lewis employs Venn diagrams to summarize the variables involved in the selection of explanations for illness as these are advanced in actual case histories. This provides an admirably succinct method of presenting complex data and could be used to collect and store directly comparable material. If this meth-

odological innovation were widely adopted and applied with sufficient
sensitivity and discrimination, it might even in time lead to the establishment of quantifiable differences in explanatory systems.

Chapter 2: Possession cults in context

1. For an admirably comprehensive bibliography of works published prior
   to 1950, see Bouteiller (1950: 327–65); for more recent material, see
   Zaretsky and Shambaugh (1978).
2. Cf. Firth's wide-ranging discussion of the effects and implications of
   the observer's personal bias in religious sociology (Firth 1959).
3. White suggests that the high incidence of these possession afflictions
   among Luvale women is, in this context, connected with the practice
   of virilocal marriage, which separates a wife from her natal kin and
   prevents her from regularly participating in offerings made to her own
   ancestors (White 1961: 48). These spirit-possession afflictions have
   thus had the effect of reminding women of their kin allegiances and
   thereby helping to maintain matrilineal solidarity.
4. For a fuller discussion see Lewis (1969).
5. The transition from the rigid traditional attitude to the modern explicit
   recognition of love is clearly shown in many of the poems of Ilmi
   Bownderi (c. 1908–38) who is generally regarded as the first major
   Somali poet to compose works in the classical style treating this theme
   directly. The following lines addressed to the woman he loved but who
   would not marry him refer directly to the forms of possession discussed here:

   > Rapt in deceitful trance, I thought that I was sleeping with her,
   > But it was only a jinn counterfeiting her image,
   > I tried to catch her by the hand, but the place beside me was empty.
   > When I discovered that it was alone I was striving,
   > I woke up abruptly, having tossed from side to side,
   > And like a prowling lion, I rumpled my bed clothes,
   > Attacking and pounding them, as if it were they who had caused
   >   my deprivation
   > And like a hero against whom men have combined to oppose, I
   >   covered my face,
   > I was humbled like the boy who, guarding his people's camels, has
   >   them seized from him,
   > I felt disgraced like a woman to whom the words "I divorce you"
   >   had been spoken,
   > It is degrading to yearn for what you cannot have,
   > Alas, alas, how disaster has overtaken me.
   >   [Abdillah and Andrzejewski, 1967]

6. Following Trimingham (1959: 31ff.) I use the word "cleric" as a general term for various Muslim holy men and religious functionaries who,

though not necessarily part of any ecclesiastical hierarchy, figure so prominently in all Islamic societies.

7. For fuller details on the procedure of exorcism see Lewis (1969).

8. There are obvious analogies here with such exotic phenomena as the so-called *"Wiitiko* psychosis" found amongst Cree and Ojibwa Indians in the northern forestland of Canada. Like the Somali camel boys' *sar,* this affliction mainly affects men, and in this case those who have spent long periods alone in the frozen forest in an unsuccessful quest for food (Parker 1960: 603). Whatever its psychological status, this appears to be a parallel cultural phenomenon, associated with physical and social isolation and deprivation, and explained in terms of possession by a monster spirit called *Wiitiko.*

9. For accounts of these in the Sudan and north Africa, see Tremearne (1914) and Westermarck (1926).

10. The best published sources for the *bori* cults are Tremearne (1913; 1914), Greenberg (1946), Mary Smith (1954), and M. G. Smith (1957; 1962).

11. Michael Onwuejeogwu, personal communication. I am also grateful for helpful comments from F. W. Parsons and Malam Esa of the School of Oriental and African Studies, London.

12. Wallace (1961) argues that Arctic hysteria (in some areas called *pibloktoq*) is the result of calcium deficiency in the Eskimo diet. This view, however, does not satisfactorily account for the differential sex incidence of the affliction. Wallace's assertion that the syndrome is not explained by the Eskimos themselves in terms of spirit-possession appears to contradict the evidence presented by Czaplicka and other authorities.

13. Colson (1969).

14. Cf. Leach (1961) and Lewis (1965).

15. Wallace (1959) has most interestingly argued that prevailing trends in psychotherapy may be related to sociocultural factors. In social systems with a "high level of organization" the emphasis in therapy tends to be on expressive catharsis, whereas in those with a "low level of organization" the bias is toward control therapy (with ego or superego reinforcement). Thus, according to Wallace, in traditional Iroquois society prior to 1650 therapy was mainly of the expressive kind associated with shamanistic rituals. Two hundred years later, however, after the misery and dislocation associated with colonization, the emphasis had shifted toward "control" psychotherapy associated with puritanical prophetic movements in which confession played an important part.

16. See, e.g., Fortes (1959), Horton (1961), and Wallace (1961: 281ff.).

17. Prominent among recent synoptic treatments of the subject are Thrupp (1962) and Lanternari (1963).

18. For a recent study of shamanistic practices associated with healing in

rural France see Bouteiller (1950: 1999–248) and in rural Italy, Penna (1963).

19. See Shepherd et al. (1964) and Shepherd (1981). This differential sex incidence is also evident, though less extreme, in the registrar general's figures for hospitalization in cases of mental illness in England. On the basis of the 1959 figures, Little (1965) has calculated expectancy rates indicating that 7.4 percent of men and 11.1 percent of women can expect to be admitted to a mental hospital for treatment once during their lives.

Chapter 3: Witchcraft within and without

1. Although very little is generally known of the history of peripheral possession cults in traditional societies, most observers of these cults, at least in Africa, report that they have arisen within this century. Since (almost invariably) they predominantly involve women and clearly operate to some extent as women's protest movements, it seems probable that they reflect changing aspirations and attitudes toward their traditional status on the part of women. Thus, as the character of the spirits themselves suggests, they seem to be responses to social change and perhaps often direct reactions to the diffusion of modern views on the social role of women. Certainly, contrary to Wilson's unconvincing assertions concerning the allegedly complete socialization of women in traditional roles (Wilson 1967), in many cases there is direct evidence of spirit-possessed women seeking to assume male roles – roles that they specifically covet and their exclusion from which they explicitly resent. For particularly clear evidence of this see Harris (1957).

2. For a detailed discussion see Beattie (1969).

3. Cf. R. Turner (1970).

Chapter 4: The cannibal's cauldron

1. See A. Dubb, ed. (1960: 145ff.).

2. Arab sources have indeed claimed that during the Crusades, Christian forces actually practiced cannibalism, eating their defeated foes as a final act of humiliation. (See A. Maalouf 1984.)

3. Professor Chavunduka is also president of the Zimbabwe National Healers Association (ZINATHA), formed with the collaboration of the minister of health in 1980.

4. For interesting treatments of these themes by contemporary east African writers see Grace Ogot's novel *Land Without Thunder* and Alumidi Osinya's *Field Marshall Abdulla Salim Fisi (or How the Hyena Got His!)*. In the latter work, an Orwellian account of the recent history of Uganda, Amin and his ethnic supporters are depicted as hyenas who successfully wrest power from the leopards (Obote's people) who rule the game park (= Uganda). Forbidden by their leader to eat other animals, the hungry leopards are clandestinely supplied with human corpses by their friends the whites. The hyena regime quickly reverses

this "animal law" and takes advantage of the devastations caused by a severe drought in the park, which makes large numbers of enfeebled animals easy prey for the hyenas.

5. See, e.g., Mary Douglas (1967: 37; 1966: 101ff.).
6. See *Nuer Religion* (1956), whose index contains no entry under "skepticism," a term that figures prominently in the Zande book.
7. Arens does, of course, recognize the occurrence of "crisis cannibalism," when starvation drives people to eat human flesh.
8. Sahlins (1983: 88).
9. See, e.g., Elsdon Best (1902).
10. This seems also to be the general conclusion reached by other Amazonian Indian specialists – e.g., Dr. S. Dreyfus-Gamelon, Dr. Joanna Overing, and Dr. Peter Rivière (personal communications).
11. Joseph Tubiana reports (personal communication) that in Ethiopia to "give someone a village to eat" signifies granting the person concerned the right to tax (and live off) the village in question. Among the Zaghawa, Marie-José Tubiana has recorded, political usurpation may be represented as a process of seduction with the aid of tempting food.
12. See Ernest Jones (1949: 120).
13. See "Cannibal of the Bois de Boulogne," *The Observer*, June 21, 1981. This case has potentially wider symbolic reverberations; the gruesome incident has been made the subject of a best-selling novel by the Japanese playwright Juro Kara, which won a prestigious Japanese literary award in 1983. Some commentators have interpreted the book as displaying the vengeance of a small Oriental who feels he is the victim of white oppression.

Chapter 5: The shaman's career

1. See, e.g., A. Hultkrantz (1973) and A. L. Siikala (1978).
2. For recent studies by contemporary Soviet scholars see V. N. Basilov (1981; 1984). For the work of Hungarian scholars see V. Voigt (1977), V. Dioszegi (1968), and M. Hoppal (1984).
3. See, e.g., A. Lommel (1965).
4. Here, however, in addition to the strong tradition of specialists working on Siberian and Mongolian shamanism (e.g., Lot-Falck, and more recently Hamayon), it is important to note the work of M. Leiris (1958; 1980). Although dealing only with Ethiopia, M. Leiris was one of the first to point to the importance of shamans and shamanism in Africa in general – a region explicitly omitted in Mircea Eliade's magisterial work, which though first published in French in 1951 and dedicated to the author's "French masters and colleagues," is left oddly unmentioned by Leiris.
5. See E. de Martino (1948). This point was made forcefully and elegantly in "Shamanism: History, Limits and Prospects for Research in Italy" (paper presented by Romano Mastromattei at the symposium, The Comparative Study of the Early Forms of Religion: Shamanism in

Eurasia; Sarospatak, Hungary, September, 1981). With his notion of spirits as hypotheses, Shirokogoroff in my opinion also anticipates many of the ideas of the contemporary English anthropologist Robin Horton (1968). It would also not be an exaggeration to claim Shirokogoroff as a revolutionary pioneer of ethno-medicine. To see, as he did in 1935, that "European medicine itself is an ethnographical phenomenon" was truly remarkable. Nor is Shirokogoroff's influence limited to his publications. China's leading contemporary anthropologist, Professor Fei Xiao-Tong, was, he has told me, one of Shirokogoroff's students, and was sent by him to study anthropology with Malinowski at the London School of Economics.

6. For a recent discussion of the literature see J. G. Oosten (1980).
7. See, e.g., H. Codere (1966: 120–71).
8. In the case of the Swedish anthropologist K. E. Knutsson's (1967) brilliant analysis of Oromo religion, which is explicitly modeled on Lienhardt's Dinka study, this influence is so strong that the term *shaman* seems to have been completely exorcised, although the phenomenon is clearly present.
9. See J. T. Hitchcock and Rex L. Jones (1976) and V. Crapanzano and V. Garrison (1977).
10. This Tungus origin is generally accepted. It has also been suggested that the word may ultimately derive from the Vedic *sram*, to heat oneself or practice austerities, and *sramana*, practitioner of austerities or ascetic. According to Sir Harold Bailey (quoted in Blacker 1975: 318) the word came to Asia from India in the Shan Kingdom form *samana*, reaching China as *shamen*, and Japan as *shamon*. See also V. Voigt (1977). The distinguished authority on Tungusic languages Robert Austerlitz, however, considers the hypothesis of an Indian origin of the Tungus form "moribund" (personal communication).
11. Eliade (1951: 434). All references here are to the 1951 French edition.
12. Notably A. Lommel (1965).
13. *Der Ursprung der Gottesidee* (1912–55: xii).
14. As Anna-Leena Siikala rightly stresses in her splendid assessment of the Siberian evidence (1978: 333), such stimulants are not, of course, by any means essential.
15. For more recent work on Tungus and Siberian shamanism, see (in addition to A. L. Siikala) A. A. Anisimov in H. N. Michael, ed. (1963); and others cited in Voigt (1977); E. Lot-Falck (1953, 1973); D. Bayle, ed. (1977); V. N. Basilov (1984); and L. P. Potapov (1978). On Buryat shamanism see R. Hamayon (1978: 17–45; 1981) and C. Humphrey (1979: 235–60). On Lapp shamanism see L. Bachman and A. Hultkrantz (1978).
16. C. Blacker (1975); see also I. Hori (1968).
17. As will be evident, this definition closely follows Shirokogoroff.
18. M. Eliade (1951), especially Chapter 4.
19. A. L. Siikala (1978: 335–6): "Since shamanic seances are for the most

part precisely healing events, it is scarcely a coincidence that basically parallel spirit and demon possessions appear in the same regions. Thus the explanation for illness: 'the demon has penetrated the patient' would in turn add to the popularity of the possession type technique of shamanizing."

20. A.-L. Siikala (1978). Professor Siikala's role-taking model of shamanism refers primarily to the structure of the seance itself. Since, however, it is often observed with justice that in the seance the shaman recapitulates his original traumatic induction, one would expect to find a certain parallelism between the structure of the initiation process and that of the seance.

21. For the Malaysian pattern see, e.g., C. S. Kessler (1977), who however does not employ the term "shaman."

22. See particularly M. Leiris ([1958] 1980: 103ff.).

23. V. N. Basilov (1981).

Chapter 6: The power of the past: African "survivals" in Islam

1. Sophie Ferchiou (1972).

2. See, e.g., E. Gellner (1982).

3. See A. J. Arberry (1950: 23). In the context of Somali Islam this is discussed by B. W. Andrzejewski (1974).

4. E. Marx (1977: 29–50).

5. I. M. Lewis (1955: 56).

6. The main sources are discussed in Lewis (1971: 101–4).

7. M. Swantz (1970); see also M. Strobel (1979).

8. *The Influence of Islam on Africa* (London, Longman, 1968).

9. "Conversion reconsidered: some historical aspects of religious conversions in Black Africa," *Africa* 43 (1973).

10. See I. M. Lewis, ed. (1980a: vii, 59) and Horton (1975).

11. D. Parkin (1970; 1972).

12. U. Braukamper (1977); B. W. Andrzejewski (1975: 139–40). See also I. M. Lewis (1980b: 409–15).

13. In other contexts the word refers to immigrant groups or individuals attached to local Somali clans. It seems to have the general sense of something extraneous superimposed or grafted onto an object or person. The generic Somali term for "possession" is literally *gelid*, "entering."

14. Also known in Somali as "Ethiopian *sar*." The female cult leader is called *alaaqad*, probably derived from Amharic *alaqa*, priest. See also Giannattasio (1983).

15. Cf. I. M. Lewis (1971).

16. Compare Jon Anderson's interesting observation that in Muslim Afghanistan upwardly mobile women often adopt the veil while the "outwardly mobile" (i.e., nomadic) discard it (Anderson 1982: 397–420).

17. V. Luling (1966).

116 Notes to pp. 101–6

18. L. W. Saunders (1977); S. Morsy (1978).
19. In the Sudan, *zar* is also commonly referred to by the Arabic term *dastur*, "constitution" or "peg" – the latter word alluding to the hold the spirits exert on their human subjects. For recent accounts of Sudanese *zar*, see Samia al-Hadi al-Nagar (1980), P. Constantinides (1977), Anne Cloudsley (1983), and Ahmed Al-Shahi (1984: 28–44).
20. Often ex-slaves, widows, or divorced women.
21. Personal communication, Professor Lidwien E. M. Kapteijns.
22. It is not implied that there is always a single cult for women and men. Frequently, as to some extent in Khartoum and on Maffia Island (A. P. Caplan 1975), there are separate cults for bourgeois wives and for low status men.
23. As, e.g., in the case of the Iranian cult of those "possessed of the atmosphere" (ahl-e-Haval) by *bad* (or "wind") spirits. See D. J. Marsden (1972).
24. Although several undated manuscripts chronicling events in sixteenth-century Ethiopia refer to *zar*, the first securely dated occurrence of the word appears to be a translation produced at the beginning of the nineteenth century by an old Ethiopian from Gondar, living in Cairo – see M. Rodinson (1964: 238–45), W. G. Plowden (1868: 264ff.), and J. Borelli (1890: 133). There is no specific reference to the *zar* cult in Lane's encyclopedic *Manners and Customs of the Modern Egyptians* (1836). In Khartoum, although the term *zar* is also used, the spirits and their cult are perhaps more commonly referred to as *dastur* (cf. Arabic, "constitution"). It is thus intriguing that Lane (229ff.) should record in his day that citizens of Cairo regularly used this term to address the *jinns* that they thought filled the air. According to the late Professor Tijani al-Mahi, who conducted extensive historical and psychiatric research on the subject, *zar* came to the Sudan in 1905 and was recorded by Ali Pasha Mubarak in Egypt in the 1890s as a "calamity now spreading in our country." B. MacDonald (1911: 332) reports that *zar* was unknown in Egypt up to 1880.
25. M. Leiris (1980); J. Tubiana (1954: 76–90).
26. M. Leiris (1980: 38). Leiris (p. 58) also notes that in Gondar *zar* spirits temporarily disappeared after the death of Emperor Johannes in the Ethiopian defeat at the hands of the forces of the Sudanese Mahdi at the battle of Matamma in 1889.
27. See Chapter 2. E. A. Alpers, "Female subculture in nineteenth century Zanzibar: the Kitimiri spirit possession cult" (unpublished manuscript), offers a similar interpretation of the expansion of this cult, which has Ethiopian connections, at a time of increasing Islamic orthodoxy.
28. See E. Westermarck (1926, vol. 1: 395–6), V. Crapanzano (1973), D. F. Eickelman (1981), and R. Jamous (1981).
29. This is, of course, equally true of the interplay between center and periphery in other world religions and ideologies, processes that in the

Indian Hindu context have been well analyzed by McKim Marriott (1955) in terms of "parochialization" (of the great tradition) and "universalization" (of the little tradition). For a valuable recent discussion of these issues in Islam, see D. Eickelman (1983: 1–16).

Bibliography

'Abdillah, M. F. and Andrzejewski, B. W. 1967. "The life of 'Ilmi Bown-deri, a Somali poet who is said to have died of love." *J. Folkl. Inst.* 4, no. 2/3: 191–206.

Aberle, D. F. 1952. "Arctic hysteria and *latah* in Mongolia." *Trans. N.Y. Acad. Sci.*, ser. 2, no. 14: 291–7.

Agar, M. H. 1982. "Towards an ethnographic language." *American Anthropologist* 84, no. 4: 779–95.

Alexandre, P. 1974. "On some witches and a predicant." In *Choice and Change: Essays in Honour of Lucy Mair,* ed. J. Davis. London, Ath-lone Press.

al-Nagar, Samia al-Hadi. 1980. "Zaar Practitioners and Their Assistants and Followers in Omdurman." In *Urbanization and Urban Life in the Sudan,* in V. G. Pons, ed. University of Khartoum, Development Studies and Research Centre.

Alpers, E. A. 1981. "Female subculture in nineteenth century Zanzibar: the Kitimiri spirit possession cult." Unpublished ms. paper presented at conference on African Women in History, University of Santa Clara, May.

Al-Shahi, Ahmed. 1984. "Spirit possession and healing: the Zar among the Shaygiyya of the Northern Sudan." *Bulletin British Society for Middle Eastern Studies* 11, no. 1: 28–44.

Anderson, J. W. 1982. "Social interaction and the veil: comportment and the composition of interaction in Afghanistan." *Anthropos* 77: 397–420.

Andrzejewski, B. W. 1974. "The veneration of Sufi saints and its impact on the oral literature of the Somali people and on their literature in Arabic." *African Language Studies* 15: 15–53.

1975. "A genealogical note relevant to the dating of Sheikh Hussein of Bale." *Bulletin, School of Oriental and African Studies* 38: 139–40.

Anisimov, A. F. 1963. "The shaman's tent of the Evenks and the origin of the shamanistic rite." In *Studies in Siberian Shamanism,* ed. H. N. Michael. Arctic Institute of North America, Anthropology of the North,

Translations from Russian Sources, No. 4. Toronto, Toronto University Press.

Anonymous. 1972. *Department of Anthropology 1972–73* (pamphlet). London School of Economics and Political Science.

1981. "Cannibal of the Bois de Boulogne." *The Observer,* June 21, 1981.

Arbery, A. J. 1950. *Sufism.* London, Allen & Unwin.

Ardener, E. 1972. "Belief and the problem of women." In *The Interpretation of Ritual,* ed. J. S. La Fontaine. London, Tavistock.

Ardener, E. and S. 1965. "A directory study of social anthropologists." *British Journal of Sociology* 16, no. 4: 295–314.

Arens, William. 1979. *The Man-Eating Myth: Anthropology and Anthropophagy.* London, Oxford University Press.

Bachman, L., and Hultkrantz, A. 1978. *Studies in Lapp Shamanism.* Stockholm, Almqvist and Wiksell.

Banton, M., ed. 1965. *The Relevance of Models for Social Anthropology.* London, Tavistock.

Barclay, H. B. 1964. *Buuri al Lamaab: A Surburban Village in the Sudan.* New York, Cornell University Press.

Basilov, V. N. 1981. "Some results of the study of the vestiges of shamanism in Central Asia." International Congress of Anthropological and Ethnological Sciences, Intercongress, Holland.

1984. "The study of shamanism in Soviet ethnography." In *Shamanism in Eurasia,* ed. M. Hoppal. Gottingen, Herodot.

Bayle, D., ed. 1977. *Voyages Chamaniques: L'Ethnographie* (n.s.). Nos. 74–5.

Beattie, J. 1961. "Group aspects of Nyoro spirit mediumship cult." *Human Problems in British Central Africa (Rhodes-Livingstone Institute Journal)* 30: 11–38.

1963. "Witchcraft and sorcery in Bunyoro." In *Witchcraft and Sorcery in East Africa,* eds. J. Middleton and E. H. Winter. London, Routledge & Kegan Paul.

1966. "Ritual and social Change." *Man* 1 (n.s.): 60–74.

1969. "Spirit mediumship in Bunyoro." In *Spirit Mediumship and Society in Africa,* eds. J. Beattie and J. Middleton. London, Routledge & Kegan Paul.

Beattie, J., and Middleton, J., eds. 1969. *Spirit Mediumship and Society in Africa.* London, Routledge & Kegan Paul.

Berger, I. 1976. "Rebels or status seekers? Women as spirit mediums." In *Women in Africa,* eds. N. J. Hafkin & E. G. Bay. Stanford, Stanford University Press.

Best, Elsdon. 1902. "Notes on the art of war as conducted by the Maori of New Zealand." *Journal of the Polynesian Society* 11, nos. 41–4.

Bjerke, S. 1981. *Religion and Misfortune: The Bacwezi Complex and the other Spirit Cults of the Zinza of Northwestern Tanzania.* Oslo, Universitetsforlaget.

Blacker, C. 1975. *The Catalpa Bow*. London, Allen and Unwin.

Bloch, M., and Parry, J., eds. 1982. *Death and the Regeneration of Life*. Cambridge, Cambridge University Press.

Bohannan, P. 1957. *Justice and Judgement among the Tiv*. London, Oxford University Press.

Bohannan, P. and Dalton, G., eds. 1962. *Markets in Africa*. Evanston, Ill.: Northwestern University Press.

Borelli, J. 1890. *Ethiopie Meridionale*. Paris, Ancienne Maison Quantin.

Bourguignon, E. 1976. *Possession*. San Francisco, Chandler & Sharp.

Bouteiller, M. 1950. *Chamanisme et guerison magique*. Paris, Presses Universitaires de France.

Braukamper, U. 1977. "Islamic principalities in south-east Ethiopia between the 13th and 16th centuries." *Ethiopianist Notes* 1, no. 1: 17–56; *Ethiopianist Notes* 1, no. 2: 1–43

Brown, P., and Tuzin, D., eds. 1983. *The Ethnography of Cannibalism*. Washington, D.C., Society for Psychological Anthropology.

Buxton, J. C. 1973. *Religion and Healing in Mandari*. Oxford, Clarendon Press.

Caplan, A. P. 1975. *Choice and Constraint in a Swahili Community*. London, Oxford University Press.

Casagrande, J. B., ed. 1960. *In the Company of Man*. New York, Harper.

Casagrande, J. B., and Gladwin, T. eds. 1956. *Some Uses of Anthropology: Theoretical and Applied*. Washington, D.C., Anthropological Society.

Cerulli, E. 1923. "Note sul movimento musulmano della Somalia." *Riv. Stud. Orient* 10: 1–36.

Chavunduka, G. 1980. "Witchcraft and the law." (Inaugural lecture delivered at the University of Zimbabwe.) *Zambezia* 8: 129–47.

Clifford, J. 1983. "Power and dialogue in ethnography: Marcel Griaule's initiation." In *Observers Observed*, ed. G. W. Stocking. Madison, University of Wisconsin Press.

Cloudsley, Anne. 1983. *Women of Omdurman: Life, Love and the Cult of Virginity*. London, Ethnographica.

Codere, H., ed. 1966. *Franz Boas: Kwakiutl Ethnography*. Chicago, University of Chicago Press.

Colajanni, A. 1982. "Shamanism and social change: the killing of an Achuar shaman. Facts and interpretations." Manuscript paper, 44th Congress of Americanists, Manchester.

Colson, E. 1958. *Marriage and the Family among the Platau Tonga of Northern Rhodesia*. Manchester, Manchester University Press.

   1969. "Spirit possession among the Tonga of Zambia." In *Spirit Mediumship and Society in Africa*, eds. J. Beattie and J. Middleton. London, Routledge & Kegan Paul.

Constantinedes, P. 1977. "Ill at ease and sick at heart: symbolic behaviour in a Sudanese healing cult." In *Symbols and Sentiments*, ed. I. M. Lewis. London, Academic Press.

Crapanzano, V. 1973. *The Hamadsha: A Study in Moroccan Ethnopsychiatry.* Berkeley, University of California Press.

Crapanzano, V., and Garrison, V., eds. 1977. *Case Studies in Spirit Possession.* London, Wiley.

Crawford, J. R. 1967. *Witchcraft and Sorcery in Rhodesia.* London, Oxford University Press.

Czaplicka, M. A. 1914. *Aboriginal Siberia.* Oxford, Clarendon Press.

Davis, J., ed. 1974. *Choice and Change: Essays in Honour of Lucy Mair.* London, Athlone Press.

de Heusch, Luc. 1962. "Cultes de possession et religions initiatiques de salut en Afrique." *Annales du Centre d'Etudes des Religions,* vol. 2. Brussels, Institut de sociologie de l'université libre de Bruxelles.

1966. *Le Ruanda et la civilisation interlacustre.* Bruxelles, Institut de Sociologie de l'Université Libre.

1971. *Pourquoi l'epouser?* Paris, Gallimard.

Delaby, L. 1977. *Chamanes Toungouses.* Nanterre, Université de Paris, Laboratoire d'Ethnologie et de Sociologie Comparative, Centre d'Etudes Mongoles.

de Martino, E. 1948. *Il Mondo Magico.* Turin, Einaudi.

Devereux, G. 1956. "Normal and abnormal: the key problem of psychiatric anthropology." In *Some Uses of Anthropology,* eds. J. B. Casagrande and T. Gladwin. Washington, D.C., Anthropological Society.

1961. *Mohave Ethnopsychiatry and Suicide: the Psychiatric Knowledge and the Psychic Disturbances of an Indian Tribe.* Washington, D.C., Smithsonian Institution Bureau of American Ethnology, bulletin 175.

Dioszegi, V. 1968. *Tracing Shamans in Siberia.* Oosterhout, Anthropological Publications.

Douglas, M. 1957. "Animals in Lele religious symbolism." *Africa* 27: 46–58.

1966. *Purity and Danger.* London, Routledge & Kegan Paul.

1967. "Witch beliefs in central Africa." *Africa* 37, no. 1: 72–80.

1970. *Natural Symbols: Explorations in Cosmology.* London, Barrie & Rockliff.

Douglas, M., ed. 1970. *Witchcraft Confessions and Accusations.* London, Tavistock.

Douglas, M., and Kaberry, P., eds. 1969. *Man in Africa.* London, Tavistock.

Dubb, A., ed. 1960. *Myth in Modern Africa: The Fourteenth Conference Proceedings of the Rhodes-Livingston Institute for Social Research.* Lusaka, Rhodes Livingston Institute.

Earthy, E. 1933. *Valenge Women.* London, Oxford University Press.

Edel, M. M. 1957. *The Chiga of Western Uganda.* London, Oxford University Press.

Eickelman, D. F. 1981. *The Middle East.* New Jersey, Prentice-Hall.

1983. "The study of Islam in local contexts." *Contributions to Asian Studies* 18: 1–16.

Eliade, Mircea. 1951. *Le chamanisme et les techniques archaiques de l'ex-tase.* Paris, Librairie Payot.

Ellen, R. F., ed. 1984. *Ethnographic Research: A Guide to General Con-duct.* London, Academic Press.

Elliot, A. J. A. 1955. *Chinese Spirit Medium Cults in Singapore.* London, Athlone Press.

Epstein, A. L. 1958. *Politics in an Urban African Community.* Manchester, Manchester University Press.

   1979. "Unconscious factors in the response to social crisis: a case study from central Africa." In *The Psychoanalytic Study of Society,* vol. 8. New Haven, Yale University Press.

Evans-Pritchard, E. E. 1937. *Witchcraft, Oracles and Magic among the Azande.* Oxford, Clarendon Press.

   1951. *Social Anthropology.* London, Cohen & West.

   1956. *Nuer Religion.* Oxford, Clarendon Press.

   1965. *Theories of Primitive Religion.* Oxford, Clarendon Press.

   1965. "Zande cannibalism." In *The Position of Women in Primitive Societies and Other Essays in Social Anthropology.* London, Faber.

   1966. "Twins, birds and vegetables" (letter). *Man* 1, no. 3: 398–9.

Ferchiou, Sophie. 1972. "Survivances mystiques et cultes de possession dans le maraboutisme Tunisien." *L'Homme* 12, no. 3: 47–69.

Field, M. J. 1960. *Search for Security: An Ethno-psychiatric Study of Rural Ghana.* London, Faber.

Firth, Raymond. 1959. "Problem and assumption in an anthropological study of religion." *Journal of the Royal Anthropological Institute* 89: 129–48.

   1960. "A Polynesian aristocrat (Tikopia)." In *In the Company of Man,* ed. J. B. Casagrande. New York, Harper.

   1966. "Twins, birds and vegetables: problems of identification in prim-itive religious thought." *Man* 1 (n.s.): 1–17.

   1967. *Tikopia Ritual and Belief.* London, George Allen & Unwin.

Firth, Rosemary. 1972. "From wife to anthropologist." In *Crossing Cul-tural Boundaries,* eds. S. T. Kimball & J. B. Watson. San Francisco, Chandler.

Fisher, H. J. 1973. "Conversion reconsidered: some historical aspects of religious conversions in Black Africa." *Africa* 43: 27–40.

Forge, A. 1970. "Prestige, influence and sorcery: a New Guinea example." In *Witchcraft Confessions and Accusations,* ed. M. Douglas. London, Tavistock.

   1972. "The Golden Fleece." *Man* 7, no. 4: 527–40.

Forsyth, D. 1983. "The beginnings of Brazilian anthropology: Jesuits and Tupinamba cannibalism." *Journal of Anthropological Research* 2: 147–78.

Fortes, M. 1959. *Oedipus and Job in West African Religion.* Cambridge, Cambridge University Press.

Fortes, M., and Dieterlen, G., eds. 1965. *African Systems of Thought*. London, Oxford University Press.

Fortune, R. 1953. *Manus Religion*. Philadelphia, American Philosophical Society.

Foster, G. 1965. "Peasant society and the image of limited good." *American Anthropologist* 67: 293–315.

Fraenkel, P. J. 1959. *Wayaleshi*. London, Weidenfeld & Nicholson.

Freilich, M., ed. 1970. *Marginal Natives: Anthropologists at Work*. New York, Harper.

Freud, S. [1913] 1950. *Totem and Taboo*. London, Routledge & Kegan Paul.

Friedland, W. H. 1960. "Some urban myths in East Africa." In *Myth in Modern Africa*, ed. A. Dubb. Lusaka, Rhodes Livingstone Institute.

Geertz, C. 1984. "Distinguished lecture: anti anti-relativism." *American Anthropologist* 86, no. 2: 263–78.

Gellner, E. 1962. "Concepts and society." *Proceedings Fifth World Congress of Sociologists*, 1.

1982. *Muslim Society*. Cambridge, Cambridge University Press.

Giannattasio, F. 1983. "Somalia: La terapia Corentico-musicale del Mingis." *Culture musicale, quaderni di etnomusicologia* 2, no. 3: 93–119.

Gifford, E. W. 1929. *Tongan Society*. Honolulu, Bernice P. Bishop Museum.

Gluckman, M. 1954. *Rituals of Rebellion in South-East Africa*. Manchester, Manchester University Press.

1963. *Order and Rebellion in Tribal Africa*. London, Cohen & West.

Greenberg, J. 1946. *The Influence of Islam on a Sudanese Religion*. New York, American Ethnological Society.

Griaule, M. 1965. *Conversations with Ogotommeli*. London, Oxford University Press.

Gussow, Z. 1960. *"Pibloktoq* (hysteria) among the polar Eskimo." *Psychoanalysis and the Social Sciences*, ed. W. Muensterberger. New York, International University Press.

Hafkin, N. J., and Bay, E. G., eds. 1976. *Women in Africa*. Stanford, University Press.

Hall, T. H. 1962. *The Spiritualists*. London, Duckworth.

Hallpike, C. R. 1972. *The Konso of Ethiopia*. Oxford, Clarendon Press.

Hámayon, R. 1978. 'Le heros de service', *L'Homme* 18, no. 3/4: 17–45.

1984. "Is there a typically female exercise of shamanism in patrilinear societies such as the Buryat?" In *Shamanism in Eurasia*, ed. M. Hoppal. Gottingen, Herodot.

Harrington, C., and Whiting, J. M. 1972. "Socialisation process and personality." In *Psychological Anthropology*, ed. F. L. K. Hsu. Cambridge, Mass., Schenkman.

Harris, G. 1957. "Possession 'hysteria' in a Kenyan tribe." *American Anthropologist* 59: 1046–66.

Harris, M. 1977. *Cannibals and Kings*. New York, Random House.

Harwood, A. 1970. *Witchcraft, Sorcery and Social Categories among the Safwa.* London, Oxford University Press.

Hitchcock, J. T., and Jones, R. L., eds. 1976. *Spirit Possession in the Nepal Himalayas.* Warminster, Arris and Phillips.

Hjort, A. 1979. *Savanna Town: Rural Ties and Urban Opportunities in Northern Kenya.* Stockholm University, Studies in Social Anthropology.

Hogbin, H. I. 1934. *Law and Order in Polynesia.* London, Christophers.

Hollingshead, A. B., and Redlich, F. C. 1958. *Social Class and Mental Illness.* New York, John Wiley.

Holm, N. G., ed. 1982. *Religious Ecstasy.* Stockholm, Alonquist and Wiksell.

Hoppal, M. 1984. "Traces of shamanism in Hungarian folk beliefs." In *Shamanism in Eurasia,* ed. M. Hoppal. Gottingen, Herodot, 430–49.

Hori, I. 1968. *Folk Religion in Japan.* Chicago, University of Chicago Press.

Horton, R. 1961. "Destiny and the unconscious in west Africa." *Africa* 31: 110–16.

1968. "Neo-Tyloreanism: sound sense or sinister prejudice." *Man* 3, no. 4: 625–34.

1975. "On the rationality of conversion." *Africa* 45: 373–99.

Hsu, F. L. K., ed. 1961. *Psychological Anthropology: Approaches to Culture and Personality.* Homewood, Ill.: Dorsey Press. [See also second revised edition, 1972, *Psychological Anthropology.* Cambridge, Mass., Schenkman.]

Hugh-Jones, S. 1980. *The Palm and the Pleiades.* Cambridge, Cambridge University Press.

Hultkrantz, A. 1973. "A definition of shamanism." *Temenos* 9: 25–37.

Humphrey, C. 1979. "The uses of genealogy: a historical study of the nomadic and sedentarised Buryat." In *Pastoral Production and Society.* Cambridge, Cambridge University Press.

Hunter, M. 1936. *Reaction to Conquest.* London, Oxford University Press.

Hurgronje, S. 1931. *Mekka in the Later Part of the Nineteenth Century,* trans. J. H. Monahan. Leiden, E. J. Brill.

Huxley, A. 1952. *The Devils of Loudon.* London, Chatto & Windus.

Ivens, W. G. 1927. *Melanesians of the S. E. Solomon Islands.* London, Kegan Paul.

Jahoda, G. 1970 (a). "A psychologist's perspective." In *Socialisation: The Approach from Social Anthropology,* ed. P. Mayer. (A.S.A. monograph no. 8.) London, Tavistock.

1970 (b). "Supernatural beliefs and changing cognitive structures among Ghanaian university students." *Journal of Cross-Cultural Psychology:* 115–130.

1971. "Social-psychological reflections on religious changes in Ghana." *Religion:* 24–31.

Jamous, R. 1981. *Honneur et Baraka, les structures traditionelles dans le Rif.* Cambridge, Cambridge University Press.

Jarvie, I. C. 1983. "The problem of the ethnographic real." *Current Anthropology* 24: 313–26.

Jones, Ernest. 1949. *On the Nightmare.* London, Hogarth Press.

Junod, H. A. 1922. *The Life of a South African Tribe.* New York, University Books.

Kaberry, P. M. 1969. "Witchcraft of the sun: incest in Nso." In *Man in Africa*, eds. M. Douglas and P. Kaberry. London, Tavistock.

Karim, Wazir-Jahan. 1981. *Ma' Betisek Concepts of Living Things.* London, Athlone Press.

Karp, I., and Bird, C. S., eds. 1980. *Explorations in African Systems of Thought.* Bloomington, Indiana University Press.

Kessler, C. S. 1977. "Conflict and sovereignty in Kelantanese Malay spirit seances." In *Case Studies in Possession*, eds. V. Crapanzano and V. Garrison. New York, Wiley.

Kiev, A., ed. 1964. *Magic, Faith and Healing.* New York, Free Press of Glencoe.

1972. *Transcultural Psychiatry.* New York, The Free Press.

Kimball, S. T., and Watson, J. B., eds. 1972. *Crossing Cultural Boundaries.* San Francisco, Chandler.

Kluckhohn, C. 1944. *Navaho Witchcraft.* Cambridge, Mass., Peabody Museum.

Knutsson, K. E. 1967. *Authority and Change.* Goteborg, Etnografiska Museet.

Koritschoner, H. 1936. "Ngoma Ya Sheitani: an east African native treatment for psychical disorder." *Journal of the Royal Anthropological Institute* 66: 209–17.

Kremser, M. 1981. "Das bild der 'menschenfressenden Niam-Niam'." In Den Berichten Deutscher Forschengsreisender des 19 Jahrhunderts'. *Wiener Ethnoshistorische Blatter*, 21.

Krige, E. J. 1936. *The Social System of the Zulus.* London, Longmans.

Kriss, R., and Kriss-Heinrich, M. 1962. *Volksglaube in Bereichdes Islam.* Wiesbaden, Otto Harrassowitz.

La Fontaine, J. S., ed. 1972. *The Interpretation of Ritual.* London, Tavistock.

Lane, E. W. [1836] 1954. *Manners and Customs of the Modern Egyptians.* London, Everyman.

Lanternari, V. 1963. *The Religions of the Oppressed.* London, Macgibbon & Kee.

Larose, S. 1977. "The meaning of Africa in Haitian vodu." In *Symbols and Sentiments*, ed. I. M. Lewis. London, Academic Press.

Laubscher, B. J. F. 1937. *Sex, Custom and Psychopathology.* London, Routledge.

Leach, E. R. 1961. *Rethinking Anthropology.* London, Athlone.

1966. "Virgin birth" (the Henry Myers Lecture). *Proceedings of the Royal Anthropological Institute for 1966*: 39–49.

1970. *Lévi-Strauss.* London, Fontana.

Lee, S. G. 1950. "Some Zulu concepts of psychogenic disorder." *S. Afr. J. Soc. Res.* 2: 9–16.

1969. "Spirit possession among the Zulu." In *Spirit Mediumship and Society in Africa,* eds. J. Beattie and J. Middleton. London, Routledge & Kegan Paul.

Legué, G. 1880. *Urbain Grandier et les possédés de Loudon.* Paris, Baschet.

Leiris, M. 1938. "La croyance aux genies 'Zar' en Ethiopie du Nord." *Journal de la psychologie normale et pathologique* 25, no. 1/2: 107–25.

1958. *La possession et ses aspects theatraux chez les Ethiopiens de Gondar.* Paris, Plon. [See also second edition, 1980. Paris, Sycomore.]

Lessa, W. A., and Vogt, E. Z., eds. 1958. *Reader in Comparative Religion.* New York, Row, Peterson.

Levine, D. N. 1965. *Wax and Gold: Tradition and Innovation in Ethiopian Culture.* Chicago, University of Chicago Press.

Levine, R. 1963. "Witchcraft and sorcery in a Gusii community." In *Witchcraft and Sorcery in East Africa,* eds. J. Middleton and E. H. Winter. London, Routledge & Kegan Paul.

Lévi-Strauss, C. 1966. *Mythologiques II: du miel aux cendres.* Paris, Plon.

1970. *The Raw and the Cooked.* London: Jonathan Cape. [English translation of *Mythologiques I: le cru et le cuit.* Paris, Plon, 1964.]

1971. *Mythologiques IV: l'homme nu.* Paris, Plon.

[1963] 1977. *Structural Anthropology.* Harmondsworth, Penguin Books.

Lewis, G. 1975. *Knowledge of Illness in a Sepik Society.* London, Athlone Press.

Lewis, I. M. 1955, 1956. "Sufism in Somaliland." *Bulletin, School of Oriental and African Studies* 17, no. 3: 581–602; 18, no. 1: 146–60.

1965. "Problems in the comparative study of unilineal descent." In *The Relevance of Models for Social Anthropology,* ed. M. Banton. London, Tavistock.

1966. "Spirit possession and deprivation cults." *Man* 1 (n.s.): 307–29.

1967. "Spirits and the sex war." *Man* 2, no. 4: 626–8.

1969. "Spirit possession in northern Somaliland." In *Spirit Mediumship and Society in Africa,* eds. J. Beattie and J. Middleton. London, Routledge & Kegan Paul.

1971. *Ecstatic Religion.* Harmondsworth, Penguin Books.

1976. *Social Anthropology in Perspective.* Harmondsworth, Penguin Books.

1977. "Introduction." In *Symbols and Sentiments,* ed. I. M. Lewis. London, Academic Press.

1980(a). "Introduction." In *Islam in Tropical Africa.* London, Hutchinson. [Original publication 1966, Oxford University Press.]

1980(b). "The Western Somali Liberation Front (WSLF) and the legacy of Sheikh Hussein of Bale." In *Modern Ethiopia,* ed. J. Tubiana. Rotterdam, Balkema.

1983. "Spirit possession and biological reductionism: a rejoinder to Kehoe and Giletti." *American Anthropologist* 85, no. 2: 412–13, 416–17.

Lieban, R. 1967. *Cebuana Sorcery*. Berkeley, University of California Press.

Lienhardt, G. 1961. *Divinity and Experience: The Religion of the Dinka*. Oxford, Clarendon Press.

Lindblom, G. 1920. *The Akamba in British East Africa*. Uppsala, Appelbergs Boktrykeri Abtieblolag.

Linton, R. 1933. *The Tantala: A Hill Tribe of Madagascar*. Chicago, Field Museum of Natural History.

Little, A. 1965. "An 'expectancy' estimate of hospitalisation rates for mental illness." *British Journal of Sociology* 16: 221–31.

Littlejohn, James. 1970. "Twins, birds etc." *Bijdragen Tot de Taal-, Land-en Volkenkunde* 126, no. 1: 91–114.

Lommel, A. 1965. *Die Weltder fruhen Jager, Modizianmaner, Schamamen, Kunstler*. Munich, Staatlicher Museum fur Volkerkunde.

Lot-Falck, E. 1953. *Les rites de chasse chez des peuples siberiens*. Paris, Gallimard.

1973. "Le chamanisme en Siberie: essai de mise au point." *Asie du Sud-Est et Monde Insulindien* 4, no. 3: 1–10.

Loudon, J. B. 1959. "Psychogenic disorders and social conflict among the Zulu." In *Culture and Mental Health*, ed. M. K. Opler. New York, Macmillan.

Lowie, R. 1920. *Primitive Society*. London, Routledge.

Maalouf, A. 1984. *The Crusades through Arab Eyes*. London, Al-Saqi Books.

MacCormack, C. 1983. "Human leopards and crocodiles." In *The Ethnography of Cannibalism*, eds. P. Brown and D. Tuzin. Washington, D.C., Society for Psychological Anthropology.

Macdonald, B. 1911. *Aspects of Islam*. New York, Macmillan.

Macfarlane, A. 1970. *Witchcraft in Tudor and Stuart England*. London, Routledge.

MacGaffey, W. 1970. "The religious commissions of the Bakongo." *Man* 5: 27–30.

1972. "Comparative analysis of central African religions." *Africa* 42: 21–31.

1980. "African religions: types and generalisations." In *Explorations in African Systems of Thought*, eds. I. Karp and C. S. Bird. Bloomington, Indiana University Press.

Mair, Lucy. 1969. *Witchcraft*. London, Weidenfeld & Nicholson.

Malinowski, B. 1922. *Argonauts of the Western Pacific*. London, Routledge & Kegan Paul.

1929. *The Sexual Life of Savages*. London, Routledge & Kegan Paul.

Marriott, McKim. 1955. "Little communities in an indigenous civilisation." In *Village India: Studies in the Little Community*, ed. McKim Marriott. Chicago, University of Chicago Press.

Marsden, D. J. 1972. "Spirit possession on the Persian Gulf." *Dyn* (Journal of the Durham Anthropological Society) 2.

Marwick, M. 1952. "The social context of Cewa witch beliefs." *Africa* 22: 120–35, 215–53.

1965. "Some problems in the sociology of sorcery and witchcraft." In *African Systems of Thought,* eds. M. Fortes and G. Dieterlen. London, Oxford University Press.

1970. "Witchcraft as a social strain-gauge." In *Witchcraft and Sorcery,* ed. M. Marwick. London, Penguin.

Marx, E. 1972. "Communal and individual pilgrimage: the region of saints' tombs in South Sinai." In *Regional Cults,* ed. R. P. Werbner. London, Academic Press.

Mastromattei, R. 1984. "History, limits and prospects for research on shamanism in Italy." In *Shamanism in Eurasia,* ed. M. Hoppal. Gottingen, Edition Herodot.

Mayer, P., ed. 1970. *Socialisation: The Approach from Social Anthropology.* (A.S.A. monograph no. 8.) London, Tavistock.

Mead, M. 1972. "Fieldwork in high cultures." In *Crossing Cultural Boundaries,* eds. S. T. Kimball and J. B. Watson. San Francisco, Chandler.

Messing, S. D. 1958. "Group therapy and social status in the Zar cult of Ethiopia." *American Anthropologist* 60: 1120–7. [Reprinted in *Culture and Mental Health,* ed. M. K. Opler. New York, Macmillan.]

Metraux, A. 1959. *Voodoo in Haiti.* London, André Deutsch.

Michael, H. N., ed. 1963. *Studies in Siberian Shamanism.* (Arctic Institute of North America, Anthropology of the North, Translations from Russian Sources, no. 4.) Toronto, Toronto University Press.

Middleton, J. 1960. *Lugbara Religion.* London, Oxford University Press.

1969. "Oracles and divination among the Lugbara." In *Man in Africa,* eds. M. Douglas & P. Kaberry. London, Tavistock.

Middleton, J., and Winter, E., eds. 1963. *Witchcraft and Sorcery in East Africa.* London, Routledge & Kegan Paul.

Morsy, S. 1978. "Sex roles, power and illness in an Egyptian village." *American Ethnologist* 5, no. 1: 137–50.

Morton, A. 1973. *The Changing Position of Ethiopian Women.* Unpublished Social Science Research Council report, London.

Muensterberger, W., ed. 1960. *Psychoanalysis and the Social Sciences.* New York, International University Press.

Murphy, R. 1972. *The Dialectics of Social Life.* London, Allen and Unwin.

Nadel, S. F. 1946. "A study of Shamanism in the Nuba hills." *Journal of the Royal Anthropological Institute* 76: 25–37.

1952. "Witchcraft in four African societies: an essay in comparison." *American Anthropologist* 54: 18–29.

Needham, R. 1967. "Right and left in Nyoro symbolic classification." *Africa* 37, no. 4: 425–52.

1972. *Belief, Language and Experience.* Oxford, Basil Blackwell.

Ogot, Grace. *Land Without Thunder.* Nairobi, East Africa Publishing House.

Oosten, J. G. 1980. *The Theoretical Structure of the Religion of the Netsilik and Iglulik.* Groningen, Meppel.

Opler, M. E. 1958. "Spirit possession in a rural area of northern India." In *Reader in Comparative Religion*, eds. W. A. Lessa and E. Z. Vogt. New York, Row, Peterson.

Opler, M. E., ed. 1959. *Culture and Mental Health.* New York, Macmillan.

Osinya, Alumidi. 1977. *Field Marshall Abdulla Salim Fisi (or How the Hyena Got His!).* London, JOE Publications.

Packard, R. M. 1980. "Social change and the history of misfortune among the Bashu of Eastern Zaire." In *Explorations in African Systems of Thought*, eds. I. Karp & C. S. Bird. Bloomington, Indiana University Press.

Paques, Vivianne. 1964. *L'Arbre cosmique dans la pensée populaire et dans la vie quotidienne du nord-ouest africain.* Paris, Institut d'Ethnologie.

Parker, S. 1960. "The Wiitiko psychosis in the context of Ojibwa personality and culture." *American Anthropologist* 62: 603–23.

Parkin, D. 1970. "The politics of ritual syncretism: Islam among the non-Muslim Giriama of Kenya." *Africa* 40: 217–33.

1972. *Palms, Wine and Witnesses.* London, Intertext Books.

Pearce-Higgins, J. D. 1957. *Resurrection: A Study of the Facts.* Worthing.

Penna, R. 1963. *La tarantella Napoletana.* Naples, Rivista di Etnografia.

Plowden, W. G. 1868. *Travels in Abyssinia and the Galla country.* London, Longmans Green.

Porter Poole, F. 1983. "Cannibals, tricksters and witches." In *The Ethnography of Cannibalism*, eds. P. Brown and D. Tuzin. Washington, D.C., Society for Psychological Anthropology.

Potapov. L. P. 1978. "Altaic shamanism: an essay in historical dating." In *General Problems of Ethnography*, ed. S. A. Arutyonov. Moscow, Academy of Sciences, Institute of Ethnography.

Reichel-Dolmatoff, G. 1971. *Amazonian Cosmos.* Chicago, University of Chicago Press.

Richards, A. 1967. "African systems of thought: an Anglo-French dialogue." *Man* 2, no. 2: 286–98.

1968. "Keeping the king divine." *Proceedings Royal Anthropological Institute for 1968*: 23–36.

Rodinson, M. 1954. *Bibliotheca Orientalis*, XXI, 238–45.

Rouch, J. 1960. *La religion et la magie Songhay.* Paris, Presses Universitaires de France.

Rouget, G. 1980. *La Musique et la transe.* Paris, Gallimard.

Ruel, M. 1970. "Were-animals and the intravected witch." In *Witchcraft Confessions and Accusations*, ed. M. Douglas. London, Tavistock Publications.

Sahlins, M. 1983. "Raw women, cooked men and other 'great things' of the Fiji Islands." In *The Ethnography of Cannibalism*, eds. P. Brown

& D. Tuzin. Washington, D.C., Society for Psychological Anthropology.

Saunders, L. W. 1977. "Variants in Zar experience in an Egyptian village." In *Case Studies in Possession,* eds. V. Crapanzano and V. Garrison. London, Wiley.

Schmidt, Pater W. 1912–54. *Der Ursprung der Gottesidee: eine historisch-kritische und positive Studie.* Munster, Aschendorffsche Verlagsbuck-handlung.

Seymour-Smith, C. 1984. "Politics and ethnicity among the Peruvian Jivaro of the Rio communities." Unpublished Ph.D. thesis, University of London.

Shack, W. 1966. *The Gurage.* London, Oxford University Press.

Shepherd, M. 1981. *Psychiatric Illness in General Practice.* London, Oxford University Press.

Shepherd, M.; Cooper, B.; Brown, A. C.; and Kalton, G. W. 1964. "Minor mental illness in London: some aspects of a general practice survey." *British Medical Journal* 2: 1359–63.

Shirokogoroff, S. M. 1935. *The Psychomental Complex of the Tungus.* London, Kegan Paul.

Siikala, A. L. 1978. *The Rite Technique of the Siberian Shaman.* Helsinki, FF Communications.

Skinner, E. P. 1966. "Islam in Mossi society." In *Islam in Tropical Africa,* ed. I. M. Lewis. London, Oxford University Press.

Smith, M. G. 1957. "Social functions and meaning of Hausa praise-singing." *Africa* 27: 26–41.

1962. "Exchange and marketing among the Hausa." In *Markets in Africa,* eds. P. Bohannan and G. Dalton. Evanston, Ill., Northwestern University Press.

Smith, Mary. 1954. *Baba of Karo.* London, Faber & Faber.

Spiro, M. E. 1968. "Virgin birth, parthenogenesis and physiological paternity, an essay in cultural interpretation." *Man* 3, no. 2: 242–61.

Stayt, H. 1931. *The BaVenda.* London, Oxford University Press.

Sternberg, L. 1924. "Divine election in primitive religion." *Proceedings of the 21st American Congress* 2: 472–512.

Stewart, K. 1946. "Spirit possession in native America." *South Western Journal of Anthropology* 2: 323–39.

Stocking, G. W., ed. 1983. *Observers Observed.* Madison, University of Wisconsin Press.

Strathern, A. 1982. "Witchcraft, greed, cannibalism and death: some related themes from the New Guinea Highlands." In *Death and the Regeneration of Life,* eds. M. Bloch and J. Parry. Cambridge, Cambridge University Press.

Strobel, M. 1979. *Muslim Women in Mombasa 1890–1975.* New Haven, Yale University Press.

Swantz, M. 1970. *Ritual and Symbol in Transitional Zaramo Society.* Uppsala, Gleerup.

Thomas, K. 1971. *Religion and the Decline of Magic.* London, Allen Lane.

Thrupp, S. L., ed. 1962. *Millennial Dreams in Action*. The Hague, Mouton.

Tremearne, A. J. N. 1913. *Hausa Superstitions and Customs*. London, John Bale.

1914. *The Ban of the Bori: Demons and Demon-Dancing in West and North Africa*. London, Heath, Cranton & Ouseley.

Trimingham, J. S. 1959. *Islam in West Africa*. Oxford, Clarendon Press.

1968. *The Influence of Islam on Africa*. London, Longman.

Tubiana, J. 1954. "Un culte des genes agrestes en Ethiopie." *Rassegna di Studi Etiopici* 13: 76–90.

Turner, R. 1970. "Witchcraft as negative charisma." *Ethnology* 9: 366–72.

Turner, V. W. 1960. "Muchona the hornet, interpreter of religion." In *In the Company of Man*, ed. J. B. Casagrande. New York, Harper.

1967. *The Forest of Symbols*. Ithaca, Cornell University Press.

1969. *The Ritual Process: Structure and Anti-Structure*. London, Routledge & Kegan Paul.

Voigt, V. 1977. "Shamanism in Siberia," *Acta Ethnographica* 26: 385–95.

Wallace, A. F. C. 1959. "The institutionalization of cathartic and control strategies in Iroquois religious psychotherapy." In *Culture and Mental Health*, ed. M. K. Opler. New York, Macmillan.

1961. "Mental illness, biology and culture." In *Psychological Anthropology*, ed. F. L. K. Hsu. Homewood, Ill., Dorsey Press.

Watson, W. 1958. *Tribal Cohesion in a Money Economy*. Manchester, Manchester University Press.

Werbner, R. P. 1964. "Atonement ritual and guardian-spirit possession among the Kalanga." *Africa* 34: 206–22.

Westermarck, E. A. 1926. *Ritual and Belief in Morocco*. (2 vols.) London, Macmillan.

Weyer, E. M. 1932. *The Eskimos: Their Environment and Folkways*. New Haven, Yale University Press.

Whisson, M. G. 1964. "Some aspects of functional disorders among the Kenya Luo." In *Magic, Faith and Healing*, ed. A. Kiev. New York, Free Press of Glencoe.

White, C. M. N. 1961. *Elements in Luvale Beliefs and Rituals*. (Rhodes-Livingstone Institute paper no. 32.) Lusaka, Rhodes-Livingstone Institute.

Whyte, S. R. 1981. "Men, women and misfortune in Bunyole." *Man* 16: 350–66.

Wilson, M. 1951. *Good Company: A study of Nyakyusa Age-Villages*. London, Oxford University Press.

Wilson, P. J. 1967. "Status ambiguity and spirit possession." *Man* 2 (n.s.), no. 3: 366–78.

1967. "Spirits and the sex war." *Man* 2 (n.s.), no. 4: 628–9.

Worsley, P. 1957. *The Trumpet Shall Sound: A Study of "Cargo" Cults in Melanesia*. London, MacGibbon & Kee.

Wyllie, R. W. 1973. "Introspective witchcraft among the Effutu of Southern Ghana." *Man* 8, no. 1: 74–9.

Zaretsky, I., and Shambaugh, C. 1978. *Spirit Possession and Spirit Mediumship in Africa and Afro-America: An Annotated Bibliography.* New York, Garland Publishing.

Index

affliction, vii, 39, 99
  cults of, vii
  women and, viii
Africa, north, 37, 103, 105
Africans, 65, 68
Akamba, 35
Alexandre, P., 69
al-Mahi, Tijani, 116n24
al-Nagar, Samia al-Hadi, 116n19
Alpers, E. A., 116n27
al-Shahi, Ahmed, 116n19
Amazon, 67
Amazonian Indian ritual cannibalism,
  74
American Indians, 8, 9
Amharic, 100
Amin, I., 112n4
ancestor cult, 18
ancestors, 59, 61, 74
Anderson, J., 115n16
Andrzejewski, B. W., 115n3, n12
Anisimov, A. A., 114n15
anomalies, 14
anti-witchcraft movements, 46
Arabia, 47
Arabs, 66, 98, 105
  Bedouin, 96
Arberry, A. J., 96
Arctic, 78
"Arctic hysteria," 38, 111n12
Ardener, E., 108n2
Ardener, S., 108n2
Arens, W., 63, 64, 72, 73, 75, 76
atheists, 21, 26
Azande, 70

"baby-bashing syndrome," 52
Bachman, L., 114n15
Balandier, G., 68

Bale, ancient Muslim state of, 99
  Sheikh Hussein of, 98, 99
"Bantu disease," 36
Banyoro, 53
Barclay, H. B., 35
Barnard, C., 66
Barotse, 11
Bashu, 58
Basilov, V. N., 39, 81, 92
BaThonga, 36, 53
Baxter, P., 5
Bayle, D., 114n15
Beattie, J., 24, 57, 79
beliefs, 18, 20, 21
Bemba, 68
Berber, 105
Best, E., 113n9
Bimin-Kuskusmin, 73–4
Blacker, C., 87
black studies, 4
Boas, F., 78
Bohannon, P., 61
Borana, 99–100
Boran pastoralists, 5
Borelli, J., 116n24
bori cult, see cult(s)
bourgeoisie, 103
Bourguignon, E., 82, 84, 85, 86, 88
Bouteiller, M., 110n1, 112n18
Braukamper, U., 115n12
Brazil, 74
bricoleurs, 9
Buddhism, 92
Bunyoro, 57
Buriat, 92
Buxton, J. C., 83

Cairo, 35
camels, 31
Cameroon, 67

cannibalism, vii, viii, ix, 63, 64, 69, 76
  anthropologists' belief in, 70–2
  as ideology, ix
  ritual, 73, 74, 75
  witchcraft and, 67, 69
"cannibal of the Bois de Boulogne," 76
Caplan, A. P., 116n22
cargo cults, 46
Casagrande, J. B., 108n10, n13
Castaneda, C., 12
caste, 78
catharsis, 24, 111n15
cathartic dances, 36
cathartic techniques, 44
Catholic, *see* Roman Catholicism
cave art, 81
Central African Federation, 65
Cerulli, E., 35, 47
charisma, vii, 62, 72
  authority and, 93
  negative, vii
Chavunduka, G., 69, 112n3
Chinese, 27, 92
Christ, 28, 47, 60, 73
Christian, 45, 46, 53, 61, 68, 92, 103
Christian Eucharist, 73
Christianity, 46, 47, 59, 98, 99
  converts to, 73
clerics, Muslim, 34
Clifford, J., 109n24
Cloudsley, A., 116n19
Code Napoleon, 69
Codere, H., 114n7
Colajanni, A., 67
colonial exploitation, 68
Colson, E., 41
compadrazgo, 78
conflict, 40
conflict strategy, 55
Congo, 65, 70
conspicuous consumption, 101
Constantinides, P., 35, 116n19
conversion, 50, 97
Cook, Florence, 48
"cosmic tree," 92
cosmology(ies), viii, 20, 22, 34, 53, 84,
  86, 92
courtesans, 45
co-wives, 38
Crapanzano, V., 114n9
Crawford, J. R., 67
Croce, B., 78
Cromer, Lord, 102, 103, 104
Crookes, William, 24
cult(s), 42
  bori, 37, 38, 44, 45, 47, 96, 105

cannibalism and, 107
charismatic, 94, 107
deprivation, 49
ecstatic women's, 106
initiation and, 97, 99
marginal, 107
orthodoxy and, 100
peripheral, 41, 42, 92, 104
possession, 94, 97
of Sheikh Hussein, 98, 99, 100
syncretic, 9, 61, 92
witchcraft and, 107
zar (sar), 28, 31–5, 37, 44, 47, 100–
  5; *see also sar* cults
"cult of affliction," 89, 107
cultural anthropology, 78
culture and personality, 84
cursing, 61
Cushitic speakers, 99, 104
Czaplicka, M. A., 39

Darwin, C., 48
De Heusch, L., 81, 82, 83, 85, 88
de Martino, E., 78, 113n5
deprivation, 30, 32, 39, 41
Devereux, G., 76
deviants, 44, 45
Devil, 48
devils, 59
diffusionism, 10, 11, 104, 105
Dinka, 46, 78, 83, 84
Dioszegi, V., 113n2
diviner, 45, 56–9
divorce, 32
Dogon, 11, 12, 16
domestication, ix
Douglas, M., 14, 21, 83–6, 89,
  109n26, n40
Dracula, 76
dreams, 15, 16
Dreyfus-Gamelon, S., 113n10
Dubb, A., 112n1
Durkheim, E., 8, 18, 84

Earthy, E., 57
Egypt, 35, 38, 47, 101, 103
Egyptian *fellahin,* 101, 103
Eickelman, D. F., 116n28
Eliade, M., 25, 80, 81, 85, 86, 88
Ellen, R. F., 108n13
Elliott, A. J. A., 27
embourgeoisement, ix
envy, 19
epidemiology, 24, 52
  and epidemiological approach, 28
  of mental illness, 49

Epstein, A. L., 64, 65
Esa, M., 111n11
eschatology, 47
Eskimos, 38, 78, 111n12
Ethiopia, 44, 47, 59, 100, 103, 104
Ethiopians, 45
Europe, 59
Europeans
  as cannibalistic witches, 68, 69
  as cannibals, 65
  in slave trade, 66
  as vampire men, 64, 66
European spirits, 36
Evans-Pritchard, E. E., 6, 7, 10, 11, 15,
  17–20, 25, 46, 61, 70, 71, 80, 83,
  108n12, 109n28, n34, n38
exorcism, ix, 60, 89, 97
ex-slaves, 44

familiars, 27, 28, 34, 59
Fei Xiao-Tong, 114n5
female disorders, 49
feminists, 41
Ferchiou, S., 115n1
fertility, 68, 74
Field, M. J., 51
fieldwork, 1–5, 8, 13
Fiji, 74, 76
Firth, Raymond, 7, 12, 15, 20, 80, 88,
  109n29, n38
Firth, Rosemary, 5, 108n9, n11
Fisher, H. J., 97
Forde, D., 7
Forge, A., 10, 12, 109n20
Forsyth, D., 75
Fortes, M., 10, 111n16
Fortune, R., 26
fortune teller, 45
Foster, G., 66
Fox sisters, 48
Fraenkel, P. J., 65
France, 78, 112n18
Frazer, J., 15
Freedman, M., 16
Freilich, M., 108n10, n13
Freud, S., 9, 19, 44, 63
Freudian ideas, 37, 39
Friedland, W. H., 65, 66
frustration, 32, 39
Fry, P., 108n14
functionalism, 50

Galla, 35
Garrison, V., 114n9
Gellner, E., 95, 109n39
Giannattasio, F., 115n14

Giriama, 98
Gluckman, M., 11, 36, 37, 40, 109n21
goats, 31
Gondar, 103, 104, 105
Gordon, General, 102, 103, 104
Grandier, Canon Urbain, 29
Greenberg, J., 111n10
Griaule, M., 12, 13, 16, 109n24, n31
Gurage, 54
Gusii, 59
Gussow, Z., 38

Haitian voodoo, 45, 47
Hamayon, R., 114n15
Harrington, C., 109n36
Harris, G., 36, 40, 112n1
Harris, M., 77
Harwood, A., 61
Hausa, 27, 37, 38, 45, 97, 105
healer, 45
Hegel, G. W. F., 9
heresy, 106
Hitchcock, J. T., 114n9
Hogbin, I., 26
holey sprites, 37, 44
Hollingshead, A. B., 49
Holy Ghost (Holy Spirit), 24, 48, 60
homosexual males, 56
Hoppal, M., 113n2
Hori, I., 114n16
Horton, R., 111n16, 114n5
Hugh-Jones, S., 67
Hultkrantz, A., 113n1
human flesh, 65, 71, 72
Humphrey, C., 114n15
Hunter, M., 59
hunter-gatherers, 81
  child-rearing practices and, 83
Hurgronje, S., 35
Huxley, A., 29
hysterical afflictions, 49

ideology, ix, 96, 107
illness, 21, 29, 30, 37, 39, 99
incest, 56, 67
incubus, 28, 53
Indian peyote cult, 44
Indian spirits, 36
informants, 14, 17
initiation, viii, ix
interpersonal tensions, 16
Iran, 103
Ireland, 5
Islam, ix, 46, 105, 106
  African, 94
  fundamentalist, 106

Islam (*cont.*)
orthodoxy and, 106, 107
popular, 95
sociologists and, 106
Islamic Hausa, 45, 97
Italy, 78
Ivens, W. G., 26

Jahoda, G., 109n39
James, W., 14
Jamous, R., 116n28
Jeanne des Anges, Sister, 29, 30
Jesuit missionaries, 75
jinns, 95, 96
Jones, E., 76, 113n12
Jones, R. L., 114n9
Junod, H. A., 36

Kaberry, P. M., 67
Kachins, 10
Kamba, 35, 45, 53
Kapteijns, L. E. M., 116n21
Kara, J., 113n13
Karim, Wazir-Jahan, 87, 107
Kenya, 36, 57, 98, 99, 100
Kessler, C. S., 115n21
key informants, 11
Kiev, A., 16
Kimball, S. T., 5
King, Katie, 24
Kluckhohn, C., 25
Knutsson, K. E., 114n8
Koran, 34, 95, 96, 97, 106
Koritschoner, H., 36
Kremser, M., 71
Krige, E. J., 36

Lalla "Aisha," 105
Lanternari, V., 46
Leach, E., 10, 20, 109n37
Lee, S. G., 36
Leiris, M., 35, 91, 104
Lele, 14
Lenje, 53, 57
Levine, D. N., 59
LeVine, R., 59
Lévi-Strauss, C., 2, 6, 8–11, 13, 20, 23,
42, 67, 108n4, n5, n6, n10, n16
Leviticus, 14
Lewis, G. A., 21, 109n41
Lewis, I. M., 50, 51, 72
Lieban, R., 59
Lienhardt, G., 46, 79
"limited good," 66
Lindblom, G., 36
lineages, 10

literacy, 106
Little, A., 112n19
Littlejohn, J., 109n38
Lommel, A., 113n3
Lot-Falck, E., 113n4
Loudon, J. B., 36
Lowie, R., 9, 108n18
Lugbara, 53, 55, 56, 61
Luling, V., 115n17
Luo, 53, 57

MacCormack, C., 67
MacDonald, B., 116n24
MacFarlane, A., 17
MacGaffey, W., 61
magic, 18, 19, 96, 107
Magreb, 105
Mair, L., 53
Malawi, 65
Malaya, 5, 107
Malinowski, B., 1, 2, 3, 6, 7, 19, 23,
28, 73
mana, 78
Manchu, 92
Mandari, 83, 84
Manus, 26
Maori, 74
maraboutism, 94, 95, 106
marginality, 94, 104
Marquesas, 73
Marriott, M., 117n29
Marsden, D. J., 116n23
Marwick, M., 25, 55
Marx, E., 115n4
Marx, K., 9
Marxist ideas, 23
Masai, 35
Mastromattei, R., 113n5
Mead, M., 4, 108n8
Mecca, 35, 96, 104
mediator, 45
mediums, 25, 27, 37, 87, 88
Malaysian *bomoh* shamans and, 90,
91
Melanesia, 73
Menelik, 104
mengis, 100
messianic cults, 24
Messing, S., 28, 35, 44
Metraux, A., 45
Michael, H. N., 114n15
Middleton, J., 56
misfortune, 21, 39
Mohammed, 28, 106, 107
moral code, 42
morality, 35, 45, 47

moral order, 46
moral values, 56
Morocco, 105
Morsy, S., 116n18
Morton, A., 91
mortuary rites, 73
Mossi, 98
Mubarak, Ali Pasha, 116n24
Murdock, G. P., 82
Murphy, R., 9
Muslim(s) (*see also* Islam), 30, 45, 98, 103
    Ethiopian, 99
Muslim clerics, 34, 95
mystical attack, 60
mystical beliefs, 15, 71
mystical experience, 88
mystical malevolence, 17
mystical power, ix, 34, 76
mysticism, 23

Nadel, S. F., 39, 40, 43, 53, 79, 80
Nasser, Gamal Abdel, 102
"natural" symbols, 72
Ndembu, 12, 14, 15, 64
Needham, R., 109n39
neurotic disorders, 49
"New Ethnography," 3
New Guinea, 10, 12, 21, 26, 73
Nicholas, Saint, 92
Nigeria, 67, 105
Nilotic peoples, 83, 85, 104
nomadic hamlets, 31
nomads, 28, 101
Nuba hills, 53, 79
Nuer, 7, 10, 20, 46, 70, 80, 84
Nupe, 39
Nyakyusa, 61, 67
Nyasaland, 65
Nyima, 53

Obote, M., 112n4
Oedipus, 63
Ogot, Grace, 112n4
Ogotommeli, 12, 13, 16
Old Testament, 46, 47
Onwuejeogwu, M., 111n11
Oosten, J. G., 114n6
Opler, M., 44
oracles, 56
"oral sadism," 76
Oromo, 99, 100
orthodoxy, ix
Osinya, A., 112n4
Overing, J., 113n10

Packard, R. M., 58
paleolithic cave art, 81
pangolins, 14
Paques, V., 92
Parker, S., 111n8
Parkin, D., 115n11
Parsons, F. W., 111n11
patient, 6
patrilineage, 74
Pearce-Higgins, J. D., 24
Penna, R., 112n18
Penthouse, 75
peripheral cults, 41, 42, 106
peripheral spirit-possession, 52, 56, 59
peyote cult, 44
plagiarism, 11
Playboy, 75
Plowden, W. G., 116n24
pollution, 73
polygyny, 32
Polynesia, 26
Pondo, 53, 59
Porter Poole, F., 73, 74, 76
possession, 42
    attitudes toward, 84, 85
    ecstasy and, 92
    peripheral, 49, 54
    primary-phase, 58, 60
    secondary-phase, 58
    shamanism and, 80, 91
    soul flight and, 92
    trance and, 87, 90
possession-afflictions, 55
potlatch, 78
praise songs, 45
priests, 52
"primitive" thought, 20
projection, 50
prophets, 46, 52
psychiatry, 5, 50
    psychiatrists and, 6, 16
    psychodynamic approach and, 16, 19
psychoanalysis, 5, 48, 49
psychoanalysts, 6
psychological illness, 49
psychology, 50
    transcultural, 49
psychosomatic disorders, 49
psychotherapy, 111n15

Quran, *see* Koran

Radcliffe-Brown, A. R., 23, 40, 50
Ramadan, 102
Redlich, F. C., 49
Reichel-Dolmatoff, G., 67

reification, ix, 107
"religions of the oppressed," 46
religious orthodoxy, 94, 95
Rhodesia
    Northern, 65, 66
    Southern, 65
Richards, A., 3, 68
ritual drama, 27
ritual rebellion, 42
Rivière, P., 113n10
Rodinson, M., 116n24
Roman Catholicism, 28, 29
romantic love, 29
Rouch, J., 37
royal power, 61
Ruel, M., 51

sacrificial communion, 73
Sahlins, M., 72, 73, 74, 76
sar, see cults, *zar (sar)*
Satan, 48
Schmidt, Pater W., 81
self-accusations, 51
Seligman, C. G., 1
Semitic cultures, 104
sex appeal, 68
sexual aggression, ix, 76, 101
sexual intercourse, 7, 28, 32, 75
sexuality, 75
    political, 68
sex war, 34, 35, 40, 47
Seymour-Smith, C., 67
shamanism, vii, ix, 53, 79, 80
    in Siberia and Mongolia, 113n4
shamans, 7, 23, 25, 32, 37, 45, 67, 78,
    79, 85, 86
    cannibalism and, 90, 94
    charisma and, 94
    clairvoyance and, 82
    "counter-roles" of, 91
    initiation of, 89
    prophets and, 88
    seances and, 92
    Shinto-Buddhism and, 87
    spirit-possession and, 88
    trance and, 82
Shambaugh, C., 110n1
Shepherd, M., 112n19
Shirokogoroff, S. M., 78, 84, 85, 86,
    88, 90, 91, 92
Shona, 40, 67
Siberia, 38, 78
Siikala, Anna-Leena, 87, 89, 91
skepticism, 18, 19, 33, 70, 95
Skinner, E. P., 98
slave trade, 66, 104

Smith, M. G., 111n10
Smith, Mary, 27
social tension, viii
Somali, 7, 17, 18, 28, 29, 30, 32, 33,
    35, 44, 45, 96, 99, 100
Somalia, 47, 99, 103
Songhay cult, 37, 45
sorcerers, 58
sorcery, 32, 33, 39, 40, 54, 56, 70, 96
South America, 2, 78
Soviet Union, 39
"speaking with tongues," 44
spirit familiars, 53
spirit mediumship, 79, 80
spirit-possession, vii, viii, 18, 23, 26,
    32, 33, 37, 39, 40, 42, 45, 48, 50,
    52, 56, 60, 79
    authentic and inauthentic, 81
    shamanism and, 80
    spirit mediumship and, 80
spirits, 15
    cannibalistic bush, 58
    peripheral, 56
    Swahili, 36
spiritual feminist movement, 57
spiritualism, 48, 49
Spiro, M. E., 109n37
spite, 19
Stanner, W. E. H., 11, 109n22
Stayt, H., 55
Sternberg, L., 28
strategies of attack, 54
Strathern, A., 73
Strobel, M., 115n7
structural-functionalism, 10, 51, 79
structuralism, 10
subversion, 56
succubi, 53
Sudan, 35, 47, 53, 70, 79, 83, 102, 105
Sufism, 95, 96, 102
superstition, ix, 17, 100, 101
"survivals," vii, ix, 94, 96, 97, 103,
    105, 107
Swahili, 36, 98
Swantz, M., 115n7
syncretism, 96, 97; *see also* cult(s), syn-
    cretic

tabu, 78
Taita, 36, 40, 53
Tallensi, 10
Tanzania, 36
tariqas, 102
Tawney, R. H., 98
therapist, 52, 58
therapy, 60

Third World, 4
Thomas, K., 17
Tikopia, 7, 12, 15, 20
Tiv, 61, 67
tokoloshe, 36, 59
Tonga, 41, 42, 53
totem, 78
trance, 81, 82, 84, 85, 87
transference, 6
translation of culture, 11
transplant surgery, 66
transvestism, 4, 24, 28
Tremearne, A. J. N., 37, 38
Trimingham, J. S., 97
Trobriand Islanders, 19, 20, 73
Tuareg, 37
Tubiana, J., 113n11
Tubiana, M.-J., 113n11
Tungus (*see also* Siberia), 80, 84–8
  cosmology of, 86, 92
Tunisia, 38, 100
Tupinamba, 74, 75
Turner, V. W., 12, 14, 89
Tylor, Edward, 15

Uganda, 56
'ulama, see Muslim clerics

vampire, 76
vampire Europeans, 64, 65, 66
Van Gennep, A., 97
Venda, 53, 55
Victorian era, 48
"Virgin Birth," 20
Voigt, Vilmos, 78
voodoo, 45, 47, 61, 78

Wallace, A. F. C., 111n12, n15, n16
Wanyika, 35
Watson, W., 58
Weber, M., 98
Werbner, R. P., 40
Westermarck, E. A., 111n9
Whisson, M., 57
White, C. M. N., 27
Whiting, J. W. M., 109n36
Whyte, S. R., 58

"wicked mother," 52
Wilson, M., 61
Wilson, P. J., 101
witchcraft, vii, viii, 16, 18, 19, 20, 26,
  32, 34, 39, 40, 45, 46, 50, 52, 54,
  56, 60, 66, 69–72, 75
  "extrovert," 52, 62
  "introspective," viii, 51, 52, 54
  shamans and, 94
  social dynamics of, 64
Witchcraft Suppression Act, 68
witch doctor, 18
witches, 58, 59
witch finders, 52
witch stereotype, 67
women, 14, 29, 44, 52
  as brides, 35
  as co-wives, 38
  ecstatic cults and, 106
  as female sheikhs, 102
  liberation of, 18
  Luvale, 110n3
  Muslim, 104
  orthodoxy and, 104
  position of, 43, 97
  roles of, 27
  Somali, 101
  as wives, 33, 34, 41, 106
world religions, ix, 97, 107
  "great" and "little" traditions in, 95,
  106
world view, 20, 53
Wyllie, R. W., 51, 52

Yako, 7
Yamani, Sheikh, 102

Zaire, 58
Zambia, 41, 64, 68
Zande, 7, 11, 17, 18, 19, 71
Zaramo, 97
zar cult, *see* cult(s), *zar* (*sar*)
Zaretsky, I., 110n1
Zimbabwe, 65, 69
zombies, 61
Zulu, 11, 36, 45, 53